The Best Birthday Parties EVer!

A Kid's Do-It-Yourself Guide

THE BEST
BIRTHDAY PARTIES
EVER!

A Kid's
Do-It-Yourself Guide

KATHY ROSS
ART BY SHARON LANE HOLM

The Millbrook Press
Brookfield, Connecticut

To my Mom and Dad, who always gave
us great birthday parties, and to
Jeannie, Bootsie, and Ricky, who were
right there with me and still are!
K.R.

To Alexandra Grace Dawes—
welcome to the world, little one!
S.L.H.

01B83
Library of Congress Cataloging-in-Publication Data
Ross, Kathy (Katharine Reynolds), 1948-
The best birthday parties ever!: a kid's do-it-yourself guide/Kathy Ross;
illustrated by Sharon Lane Holm.
p. cm.
Summary: Provides instructions for the invitations, games, crafts, table
decorations, and cakes for a dozen birthday parties based on such themes as
outer space, puppets, and dinosaurs.
ISBN 0-7613-1410-5 (lib. bdg.). —ISBN 0-7613-0989-6 (pbk)
1. Children's parties—Juvenile literature. 2. Birthdays—Juvenile literature.
[1. Parties. 2. Birthdays. 3. Games. 4. Handicraft.] I. Holm, Sharon Lane, ill.
GV1205.R65 1999
793.2'1—DC21 98-27503 CIP AC

Published by The Millbrook Press, Inc.
2 Old New Milford Road
Brookfield, Connecticut 06804
Visit us at our web site: http://www.millbrookpress.com

Lib: 1 3 5 4 2
Pb: 1 3 5 4 2

Contents

Introduction

If you are the kind of person who likes to make your own parties, this is the book for you! It is full of fun and simple ideas for twelve different parties, each with a special theme.

In each party chapter, you'll find an idea for an invitation, decorations for the table, a party favor and a party hat for each guest, and crafts to make and games to play at the party. You will also find an idea for an unusual cake that fits the party theme, which you and the grown-up helping you plan the party can make together.

You can make a wonderful theme party all on your own, but if you want to include a few inexpensive "store-bought" items with your party favors, you will find some ideas sprinkled into the illustrations.

So, have fun planning and preparing for your party—and have a great time at your best birthday party ever!

Kathy Ross

Three Bears Party

Celebrate your birthday with three bears—or more!

House Invitation

FOR EACH INVITATION YOU WILL NEED:
a card envelope
yellow construction paper

TOOLS: scissors, markers, white glue

A Party For Jimmy
where:
when:
time:

Come to my Three Bear Birthday Party!
Bring your favorite bear with you!

From: Jimmy Lowe
12 Rose Ave.
Sandy, PA 60211

To:
Alex Day
1 Oak Tree
Sandy, PA
60211

1 Cut a hole about 1½ by 2 inches (4 x 5 cm) out of the upper left side of the front of the envelope. This is the window of the house invitation. Outline the window with a marker.

2 Draw a door on the front of the envelope. Write your friend's name on the door. (If you are going to mail your invitation, make sure the door that you draw is big enough for your friend's name and address.)

3 Open the flap of the envelope so that it looks like the roof of the house. Cut a chimney out of the construction paper and glue it on the opened flap.

4 Cut a piece of construction paper big enough to fit exactly inside the envelope house. Put the paper inside the envelope and draw the faces of the three bears peeking out the window. Take the paper out of the envelope and finish drawing the heads and bodies of the three bears.

5 Next to the bears, write who the party is for, and where and when it will be. Also write your phone number so your friends can let you know if they can come.

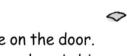

Ask your friends to bring a favorite bear to the party. Put name tags on the bears so they don't get mixed up.

bear
pompoms

8

bear bubbles

Bear Ears Party Hat

FOR EACH PARTY HAT YOU WILL NEED:
brown construction paper
wax paper
yellow paper scrap
two black and one yellow 6-inch (15-cm) pipe cleaners

TOOLS: scissors, white glue, cellophane tape,
      marker, hole punch

1 Cut a 2-inch (5-cm)-wide strip from brown paper, long enough to fit around your head. (You may need to tape two pieces together to make the strip long enough.) Tape the ends together to make a headband.

2 Cut two round bear ears from the brown paper and glue them on each side of the front of the band.

3 To make a bee to fly above the bear hat, hold a black and a yellow pipe cleaner together. Wrap the pipe cleaners around your finger to form a bee body and slide them off your finger.

4 Slip the end of the other black pipe cleaner through the bottom of the bee and bend the end to attach it. Tape the other end of the pipe cleaner behind one of the bear ears, so that it looks like the bee is buzzing around.

5 Punch eyes from yellow paper and draw a black dot in the middle of each one. Glue the eyes to one end of the bee. Cut wings from wax paper and tuck them between the two pipe cleaners at the top of the bee. Hold the wings in place with a dab of glue.

Three Bears Party Table Decorations

Cover the table with a bright-green paper tablecloth. Cut out construction-paper flowers and decorate the tablecloth by attaching them with masking tape. Use red partyware plates and cups, decorated with flower stickers.

Cut round bear ears from brown construction paper and tape two on the top back of each guest's paper plate. Set the plates face down so that guests can draw their own bear face. If you are using plastic partyware

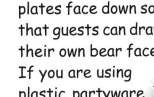

mini flower erasers

9

that is colored on both sides, put a white paper plate with ears on top of the plastic one for your guests to draw on.

Hang blue party streamers from the ceiling to make a sky.

On the day of your party, use permanent markers to draw stripes and faces on round yellow balloons. (Make the face of the bee on the bottom of the balloon.) Cut wings from wax paper and tape them on the bees' backs. Tape a piece of string between the wings. Hang several bees from the ceiling among the blue streamers.

Bear Party Favor

FOR EACH PARTY FAVOR YOU WILL NEED:
two wrapped lollipops
small plastic yogurt container
brown construction paper
black construction-paper scraps

TOOLS: scissors, white glue, cellophane tape

1 Tape a large sheet of brown paper around the yogurt container. Trim off the extra paper at the top and bottom. Make one covered container for each of your guests. If all the containers are the same size, untape this first sheet and use it as a pattern to cut the brown paper to cover the rest of the containers.

2 Tape the sticks of the lollipops inside the container on opposite sides, so that the candy tops stick out to form bear ears.

3 Cut a face from the black paper scraps and glue the face on the side of the cup.

Fill each bear cup with candy and small toys. You might want to put a marker or crayon in each cup so your guests can make the decorations on pages 9–10 for your party table.

bear rubber stamps

bear kick balls

Circle Bear Party Craft

FOR EACH BEAR YOU WILL NEED:
two different patterns of wallpaper (from old
   wallpaper book)
black construction paper
ribbon

TOOLS: a drinking cup, a large plate and
a small plate, a quarter, pen, ruler, scissors,
white glue, newspaper

 1 Prepare an area for your guests to work on by covering a large, flat table (or other surface) with newspaper.

 2 Tracing around the plates, cut a 6-inch (15-cm) and an 8-inch (20-cm) circle out of the first pattern of wallpaper to make the head and body of each bear.

 3 Tracing around the drinking cup, cut six 3-inch (8-cm) circles out of the second pattern for the ears and paws of each bear.

 4 Tracing around the quarter, cut three circles out of black paper for the face of each bear.

 5 Make one sample bear ahead of time so that everyone can see how the circles are glued together to form a bear (see the picture above).

 6 Make a pretty bow and glue it at the neck of the bear. You can tie ribbon into bows ahead of time or you can let your guests choose the ribbon they like from your birthday presents.

Circle Bear Party Game

To make this circle bear craft into a party game, give each guest the body and one paw of a bear. Hide the rest of the pieces around the room or mix them up in a big pile.

Explain to your guests that they need to find the head, paws, and ears that match the patterns on the pieces they have been given. The patterns of the head and body need to match, and the patterns of the paws and the ears need to match.

The first one to find all the pieces of a bear is the winner. When all your guests have found all their bear pieces, they can go to the work area to make bears.

Three Bowls of Porridge Cakes

String plastic beads for your bears and guests.

Bake three cakes in three graduated sizes of oven-proof bowls.

Remove the cakes from the bowls, and when they cool, cut the mound off the top of each cake to flatten it.

Frost the three cakes and decorate the sides with candies.

Wrap the handles of three plastic spoons in aluminum foil. Stick a spoon in the top of each bowl at an angle.

Your friends will think you are serving them bowls of porridge instead of birthday cakes! And all of them are just right!

Use jelly beans, round jelly candies, or licorice to decorate the bowls.

Bear Party Games

Spoon the Porridge Game

YOU WILL NEED:
- soup kettle
- serving spoon
- soup bowl
- bag of cotton balls
- blindfold
- timer

TO GET READY, dump all the cotton balls into the soup kettle. Fluff them to separate.

TO PLAY, each person gets a turn to see how much "porridge" he or she can spoon from the kettle to the soup bowl in 30 seconds. This is quite tricky when it is done blindfolded! Cotton balls are so light that it is hard to tell if you have any on the spoon if you can't see them. The winner of the game is the person who is able to spoon the largest number of cotton balls into, not all around, the soup bowl.

Bear Paws Relay Race

YOU WILL NEED:
- two pairs of heavy socks or mittens
- a piece of wrapped candy for each person (do not use hard candy)
- two bowls to hold the candy

TO PLAY, divide your party guests into two teams. If you have an uneven number of people, choose one person to go twice. At the signal to start, the first person in each line must put on the socks or mittens "bear paws," crawl to the candy dish, get a piece of candy, crawl back to the line, un-wrap the candy, and pop it in his or her mouth. This can be pretty tricky! The "paws" are then passed to the next person in line, who does the same thing. The first team to finish is the winning team.

Broken Musical Chairs

YOU WILL NEED:
- one sheet of green construction paper for each person
- markers
- music

TO GET READY, draw a simple chair shape on all the sheets of paper except one. Make sure that you cannot see the drawings of the chairs through the paper. On the last sheet of paper, draw a pile of sticks to rep-resent a broken chair. (We all know who broke it!)

TO PLAY, arrange the papers face down in a circle on the floor. There should be one paper for each person playing. The grown-up helping you with your party starts the music. Everyone walks around the papers. When the music stops, each person picks up a sheet of paper. The person who has the drawing of the broken chair is out. Take away one chair picture (not the broken chair) and put the paper face down again in a circle on the floor. Continue playing until only one player is left—the winner of the game!

Draw the Bear Game

YOU WILL NEED:
- paper for each player
- marker for each player
- 24 index cards
- paper to make a chart

TO GET READY, write the number 1 on four index cards and the number 2 on four index cards. Do the same for numbers 3, 4, 5, and 6. Make a chart to show what each number means, like this:

    #1 = head
    #2 = body
    #3 = hand paws
    #4 = foot paws
    #5 = ears
    #6 = face

Draw a bear on the chart.

TO PLAY, mix up the index cards and put them all face down on the floor. The players sit in a circle around the cards and take turns pulling a card from the pile.

The object of this game is to be the first person to draw a complete bear. The bear must be drawn in order from 1 to 6. A player who pulls a number 1 card may draw the bear's head. If the next card is not a number 2, that player's turn ends, and it's the next player's turn. Each drawn card is put back into the pile after each turn.

The first player to pull all six numbers and complete the bear picture is the winner of the game.

Pass the Bear Around

YOU WILL NEED:
- a bear for each guest (you might want to have some extra bears or other stuffed animals available to lend to any friends who forgot to bring a bear to the party or did not have one)
- music

TO PLAY, all the players sit in a circle hold-ing someone else's bear. When the music starts, the bears are passed around the circle. When the music stops, anyone holding his or her own bear is out. Continue until you have a winner—or winners. This game could have two winners, so be sure you have two prizes ready in case that happens.

Outer Space Party

Invite your friends to a party that is out of this world!

Astronaut Pass Invitation

FOR EACH INVITATION YOU WILL NEED:
a zip-to-close sandwich bag
white construction paper
blue yarn
star stickers

TOOLS: markers, scissors, hole punch

1 Cut a piece of white construction paper large enough to fit exactly inside the zip-to-close bag.

2 On the front of the paper, write "Authorized Personnel Only" and "VIP✳ Pass. " Then write "Astronaut" and fill in the name of the friend you will be giving the invitation to. Decorate with star stickers or markers.

3 On the back of the paper, write "VIP Pass for an Outer Space Birthday Party for" and write your name, address, and the date and time of your party. You might also want to write RSVP (which means "please respond") and your phone number so the people you have invited can tell you if they are able to come or not. At the bottom of the paper, write "Please wear VIP Pass for admittance."

4 Put the paper in the zip-to-close bag and seal the bag. Punch a hole at each side of the bag under the zip-top. Tie the end of a length of yarn through each hole to make a necklace so that your guests can wear their VIP Astronaut Passes to your party.

✳Very Important Person

Alien Eyes Party Hat

FOR EACH HAT YOU WILL NEED:
piece of 9- by 12-inch (23- X 30-cm) green construction paper
black and white construction-paper scraps
two 12-inch (23-cm) green pipe cleaners
two 2-inch (5-cm) Styrofoam balls
green glitter

TOOLS: white glue, scissors, cellophane tape, Styrofoam tray

1 Cut the green paper in half so that you have two strips of paper 12 inches (30 cm) long. Fold the two strips in half lengthwise to make them sturdier. Tape the ends of the two strips together to form one long strip. Wrap the strip into a band that fits around your head. Trim off any extra paper and tape the ends together to make a headband.

2 Cover the two Styrofoam balls with white glue and sprinkle them with green glitter. Let the balls dry on a Styrofoam tray.

3 Bend the two pipe cleaners in half. Stick the ends of one folded pipe cleaner into one of the green balls. Stick the ends of the other folded pipe cleaner into the other green ball.

4 Slide the folded end of the pipe cleaner between the paper strips of the headband and tape the pipe cleaner in place. Position and tape the other pipe cleaner and ball on the opposite side of the headband.

5 Cut eyes from black and white paper and glue one on the front of each green ball.

Outer Space Party Table Decorations

Use a black paper tablecloth decorated with self-stick stars or gold glitter. The glitter will be messy, but it looks great! Use yellow partyware decorated with self-stick stars.

glow-in-the-dark space balls

Hang black streamers from the ceiling with tape. Hang some colorful round balloon planets between the streamers.

Turn one or more of your small doll friends into an astronaut. Cover the face of the doll with plastic wrap to make a face mask. Then wrap the doll in aluminum foil, leaving the plastic-covered face area uncovered. Tape two film canisters to the back of the doll for air tanks. To make an air hose, insert one end of a pipe cleaner between the tanks and the other end into the face mask. Make one or more doll astronauts to hang from the ceiling. They'll look like they are taking a "space walk."

Space Walk Party Favor

FOR EACH FAVOR YOU WILL NEED:
cardboard toilet-tissue tube
aluminum foil
bathroom-size paper cup
6-inch (15-cm) square of orange tissue
6-inch (15-cm) black pipe cleaner
2-inch (5-cm)-tall astronaut sticker
   (or markers and white paper)
plastic sandwich bag

TOOLS: cellophane tape

1. To make a rocket ship, tape a paper cup over one end of the tube. Cover the ship with aluminum foil, tucking the loose ends into the open end of the tube.

2. Poke a hole in the top of the ship. Slip one end of the pipe cleaner into the hole and tape it to the inside of the tube.

3. Tape the astronaut to the other end of the pipe cleaner so that it looks like he or she is taking a space walk. If you don't have a sticker, use the markers and white paper to draw your own astronaut.

4. Put candy and prizes in a plastic sandwich bag and slide the bag into the open end of the tube.

5. Stuff the center of the orange tissue-paper square into the end of the tube so that it looks like flames are coming out of the rocket. Tape the tissue in place.

Make a rocket ship party favor for each of your guests.

red, white, or blue whistles

Comet Ball Party Craft

FOR EACH COMET BALL YOU WILL NEED:
tennis ball
aluminum foil
thin Mylar ribbon
plastic grocery bags

TOOLS: scissors, ballpoint pen

 1 Ask an adult to cut a 1-inch (2.5-cm) slit in the side of each ball.

 2 Cut strips about 1 inch wide and 1 foot (30 cm) long from the plastic grocery bags. Cut two strips for each ball.

 3 Cut pieces of Mylar ribbon about 1½ feet (46 cm) long. Cut four pieces for each ball.

 4 Make one sample comet ball ahead of time so that everyone can see how it is made. Wrap the ball in foil, leaving the slit open. Poke the ends of the plastic strips and the ribbon into the slit to make the comet's tail.

 5 Make sure there is a ballpoint pen at your party so that people can write their names on the comets they make.

Comet Ball Game

If your party is held outdoors, you can make a game out of seeing who can throw a comet the farthest. The tails look very pretty flying behind the balls.

If your party is held indoors, play "Toss the Comet in the Crater." A wastebasket makes a perfect crater. Have people take turns throwing their comets into the crater. At first, the players should stand very close to the crater. They step farther and farther back with each round. When players miss the crater, they are out of the game. Keep playing until only the winner is left.

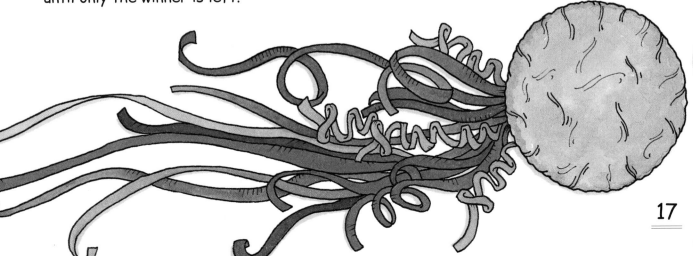

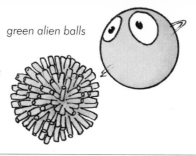
green alien balls

glow-in-the-dark
porcupine balls
for prizes

Aliens-on-the-Moon Birthday Cake

Bake your favorite flavor cake in two 9-inch (23-cm) ovenproof bowls.

Remove the cakes from the bowls and trim off the mound on one of the cakes to flatten it.

Tint white frosting gray by adding drops of red, green, and blue food coloring. Frost the flat top of the first layer, then put the second cake on top of it. Frost the top and sides of the whole cake. Press the bowl of a spoon into the frosting to make craters in the moon cake.

Make aliens out of large green gumdrops. Make their arms from tooth-pick halves and their legs from whole tooth-picks. Push two pepper-corns into each gumdrop to make eyes. Push the birthday candles into the top of each alien.

Sprinkle star stickers around cake plate.

Outer Space Party Games

Saucer Balance Game

YOU WILL NEED:
- two identical heavy paper plates for each guest
- white glue
- markers
- music

TO GET READY, glue the top edges of two paper plates together to make a saucer. Make one saucer for each person playing the game. You can decorate the saucers yourself or give your guests markers to decorate their own saucers during the party.

TO PLAY, the grown-up helping with your party plays the music. While the music is playing, everyone walks around the room balancing a saucer on his or her head. When the music stops, every-one must kneel down—carefully. Anyone who drops a saucer is eliminated. Start and stop the music until only one person is left—the winner of the game!

UFO

Rocket Race

YOU WILL NEED:
- two empty dish-detergent bottles
- piece of string or yarn
- aluminum foil
- scissors

TO GET READY, cut a rocket ship 5 inches (13 cm) tall from aluminum foil for each player.

TO PLAY, the players squeeze air from a dish-detergent bottle to blow the rocket ships across the room. Mark the finish line with a piece of string or yarn. Players may shape their foil rocket ships any way they wish before the race begins. But during the race, they cannot touch them. Players race two at a time. After everyone has played once, the winners in each pair race each other until there is only one winner left. If you collect enough empty detergent bottles, everyone at the party can race at the same time.

Toss the Ring Around Saturn

YOU WILL NEED:
- 12-inch (30-cm) paper plate for each guest
- aluminum foil
- small coffee can
- scissors
- ballpoint pen
- ball about 6 inches (15 cm) in diameter
- music
- pencil and paper
- sticker stars

TO GET READY, make a ring for each guest by cutting a 3/4-inch (2-cm) ring from the outer edge of a paper plate. Wrap each ring with foil to make it a little sturdier and heavier. With the ballpoint pen, write the name of each person who will be playing the game on one of the rings. Cover the coffee can with foil and sticker stars to make it look nice.

TO PLAY, give each person the ring with his or her name on it. Rest the ball on top of the open end of the coffee can. Have everyone form a circle around it. The ball is Saturn (but it's missing its rings). When the grown-up who is helping you with your party plays the music, everyone walks around Saturn in a circle. When the music stops, all the players toss their rings over Saturn. Check the names written on the rings that are over the ball. Each person who tossed a ring over Saturn gets one point. Use the paper and pencil to keep score. The person with the most points after ten games is the winner. If there's a tie, keep playing until the tie is broken.

Flying Saucers Match Game

YOU WILL NEED:
- at least two 6-inch (15-cm) paper plates for each guest
- two identical packages of outer space stickers (or markers and white paper)

TO GET READY, make pairs of matching plates by putting the same kinds of stickers on two different plates. If you do not have outer space stickers, draw matching pictures of stars, comets, planets, robots, rockets, and other space-related objects. You can also write matching words on the plates, such as the names of the planets.

TO PLAY, give everyone two or more plate saucers to sail around the room. At the signal "Go!" all the players must try to pick up as many saucers as they can. When all the saucers have been picked up, the person with the most matches wins. Keep re-playing ties until you have only one winner.

Planet Line-Up Relay

YOU WILL NEED:
- 18 paper plates
- markers or crayons
- paper and pencil

TO GET READY, make two sets of nine paper plates. Write the names of the planets on each set, one planet's name on each plate.

TO PLAY, divide the group into two teams. Give each team one set of the planet plates. Each player should have one or more plates so that all the planets are distributed. The grown-up helping with your party calls out the names of two or more planets. Both teams try to line up the planet plates on the floor in the order called. The team that does this first receives one point. The first team to reach ten points is the winner.

Rainbow Party

Invite your friends "over the rainbow" to a colorful party.

Round Rainbow Invitation

FOR EACH INVITATION YOU WILL NEED:
yellow and white construction paper
paper fastener

TOOLS: a saucer or small plate, markers, ballpoint pen, scissors

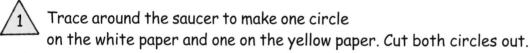

1. Trace around the saucer to make one circle on the white paper and one on the yellow paper. Cut both circles out.

2. Cut a half-circle shape inside the yellow circle.

3. Fasten the yellow circle on top of the white one by putting a paper fastener through the center of both circles.

4. Trace inside the cutout half circle onto the white paper. Unfasten the two circles. Color the traced window shape to look like a rainbow. Color the other half of the white paper to look like sky. (Don't make the sky too dark because you will need to write on it.)

5. Fasten the two circles back together. Turn the white circle around. If any white paper sticks out at the edges of the yellow circle, just trim it.

6. On the blue sky, write "You are invited to...." Below that, in parentheses, write "turn." Turn the white circle. On the rainbow, write "A Rainbow Birthday Party for" and fill in your name.

7. On the bottom of the yellow circle, write where and when the party will be held. Include the date and the time. Write RSVP (which means "please respond") and your phone number, too, so your friends can call to let you know they'll be coming.

Bluebird Party Hat

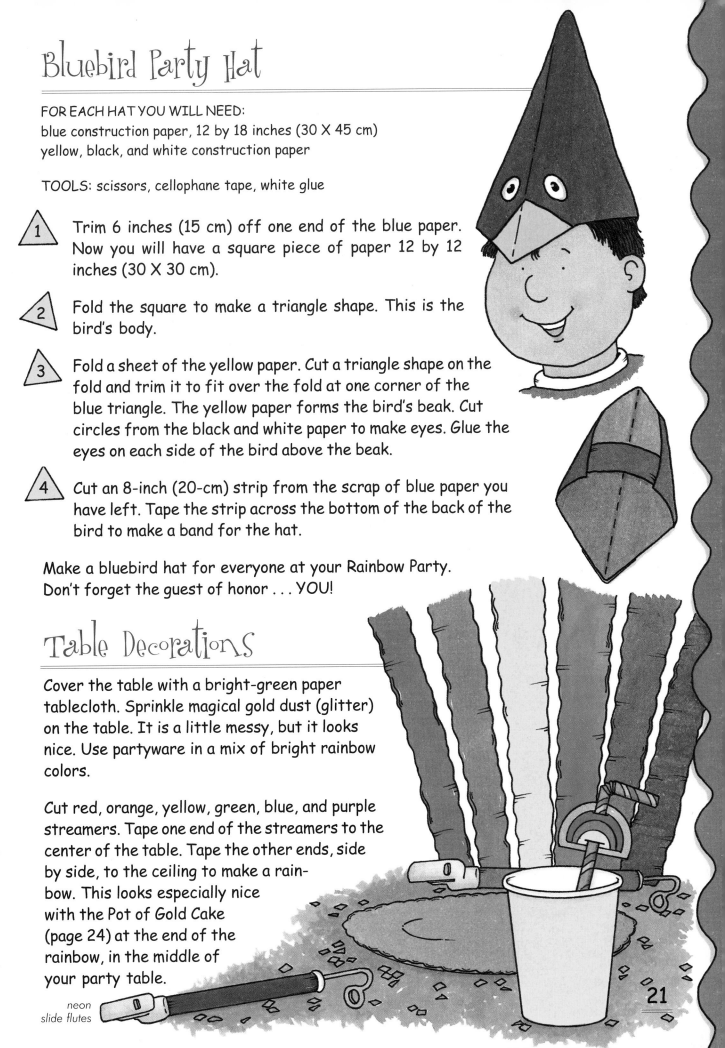

FOR EACH HAT YOU WILL NEED:
blue construction paper, 12 by 18 inches (30 X 45 cm)
yellow, black, and white construction paper

TOOLS: scissors, cellophane tape, white glue

1. Trim 6 inches (15 cm) off one end of the blue paper. Now you will have a square piece of paper 12 by 12 inches (30 X 30 cm).

2. Fold the square to make a triangle shape. This is the bird's body.

3. Fold a sheet of the yellow paper. Cut a triangle shape on the fold and trim it to fit over the fold at one corner of the blue triangle. The yellow paper forms the bird's beak. Cut circles from the black and white paper to make eyes. Glue the eyes on each side of the bird above the beak.

4. Cut an 8-inch (20-cm) strip from the scrap of blue paper you have left. Tape the strip across the bottom of the back of the bird to make a band for the hat.

Make a bluebird hat for everyone at your Rainbow Party. Don't forget the guest of honor . . . YOU!

Table Decorations

Cover the table with a bright-green paper tablecloth. Sprinkle magical gold dust (glitter) on the table. It is a little messy, but it looks nice. Use partyware in a mix of bright rainbow colors.

Cut red, orange, yellow, green, blue, and purple streamers. Tape one end of the streamers to the center of the table. Tape the other ends, side by side, to the ceiling to make a rainbow. This looks especially nice with the Pot of Gold Cake (page 24) at the end of the rainbow, in the middle of your party table.

neon slide flutes

21

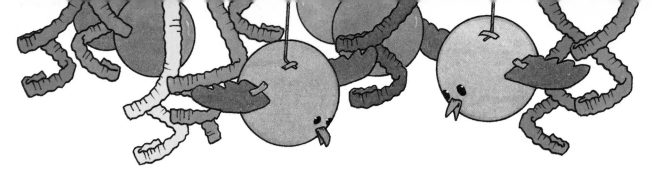

On the day of your party, make some bluebird balloons to hang from the ceiling over the party table. To make bluebird balloons, turn each balloon sideways and draw eyes on the bottom of the balloon. Cut a beak from orange paper and tape it below the eyes. Cut wings from blue paper and tape them to the back of the bird. Tape a string to the bird's back to use as a hanger.

Rainbow Basket Party Favor

FOR EACH FAVOR YOU WILL NEED:
9-inch (23-cm) paper plate

TOOLS: markers, stapler

1. Make a circle of red, about 1/2 inch (1 cm) wide, around the rim of the paper plate. Color an orange circle inside the red circle. Inside the orange circle color a yellow circle. Continue to add circles of green, blue, and purple.

2. Fold the colored plate in half to form a basket with a rainbow on each side. Staple the folded plate together on each side to hold it, but leave the top open so that you can fill the basket with candies, small toys, and other goodies.

Make a rainbow basket for each person at your party table.

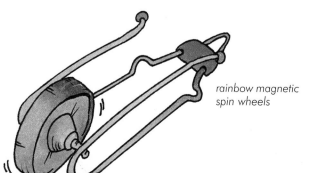

rainbow magnetic spin wheels

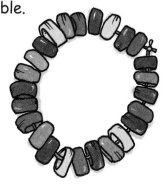

multi-colored pony beads for bracelets

Rainbow Puppet Party Craft

FOR EACH PUPPET YOU WILL NEED:
red, orange, yellow, green, blue, and purple construction paper
one half of a 9-inch (23-cm) paper plate
Popsicle stick

TOOLS: scissors, cellophane tape, white glue, markers

 1. Cut the paper plates in half so that you have half a plate for each guest.

 2. For each puppet, cut a strip of paper, 1 by 9 inches (2.5 X 23 cm), from each of the six colors of construction paper.

 3. Make one sample puppet ahead of time so that everyone can see how it is made. Fold the two sides of the paper plate together to form a pie-wedge shape.

 4. Glue the ends of the strips of paper inside the wide end of the plate. Press the front and back of the folded plate together to glue the strips in place. The colorful strips are the puppet's rainbow-colored hair.

 5. Slide the Popsicle stick inside the tip of the folded plate. Tape the stick to the plate to hold it in place. Tape the edges of the folded plate together to keep it closed.

 6. Draw a face with markers on the front of the puppet.

Rainbow Puppet Game

To play "Birds Over the Rainbow" with the rainbow puppets, give each guest a different color craft feather. Mark start and finish lines for the race with yarn. When the signal is given to "go," all the players fan their feather birds with their puppets. Whoever makes a feather bird fly over the finish line first is the winner.

mini rainbow erasers

Pot of Gold Cake

colored letter beads

Bake two cakes in identical 9-inch (23-cm) bowls (or bake the cakes one at a time in the same bowl). Remove the cakes from the bowls, and trim the mound off the top of each cake to flatten it.

Frost the flat top of one cake. Lay the flat top of the other cake on top of the first cake. Frost the whole cake. Chocolate frosting looks great on this "pot" cake.

Add strips of licorice to make handles on each side of the "pot." Cover the top of the cake with gold foil-wrapped chocolate coins or other types of gold foil-wrapped candy.

Rainbow Party Games

Find the Rainbow Colors Race

YOU WILL NEED:
- stack of colorful old magazines

TO PLAY, everyone chooses one magazine without looking inside it. When the grown-up helping you with your party signals "Go," all the players look for the six rainbow colors in pictures in their magazines. The colors must be found in order from red to purple. When the first color, red, is found, the player rips the page out of the magazine. The color red must be easy to see on the page. After finding red, the players can look for orange, yellow, green, blue, and purple. The first person to have a stack of six magazine pages, containing the six rainbow colors, is the winner.

Rainbow Hunt

YOU WILL NEED:
- yarn or ribbon in red, orange, yellow, green, blue, and purple
- scissors

TO GET READY, cut six 12-inch (30-cm) pieces of ribbon or yarn, one of each rainbow color, for each guest. If you want to play this game, too, ask the grown-up who is helping you with the party to hide all the pieces of yarn or ribbon around the room.

TO PLAY, each player tries to make a complete rainbow by finding all six colors of yarn. Each player may pick up only one of each color. The first person to find a complete rainbow is the winner, but it is fun to continue to play until all the players have found all the pieces of their rainbows.

Gold in the Pot Game

YOU WILL NEED:
- soup kettle
- pie tin
- ten pennies or ten gold foil-wrapped coins
- yarn in red, orange, yellow, green, blue, and purple

TO GET READY, make a pretty rainbow line for the players to stand behind. Cut strands of yarn 4 feet (120 cm) long in each of the six rainbow colors and knot the strands together at the two ends. Turn the kettle—your pot of gold—upside down and set the pie tin on top. As you and your guests will see, it is much harder to toss coins into a pie tin than into the deep open kettle.

TO PLAY, each player takes a turn standing behind the rainbow line and tossing ten coins into the pie tin. The person who gets the most coins in (the coins also have to stay in) is the winner. If there is a tie, the tied players should play again until one winner is left.

Pass the Rainbow Surprise Ball

YOU WILL NEED:
- rolls of red, orange, yellow, green, blue, and purple streamers
- a small prize
- cellophane tape
- music

TO GET READY, wrap the prize several times in the roll of purple paper. Next wrap it in blue, then green, then yellow, then orange, and finally in red paper. Tape the end of the red streamer with a small piece of tape. Wrapping takes a while, so you might want to start the job a few days before your party, finishing one roll each day.

TO PLAY, all the players should sit in a circle. Untape the end of the red streamer of the surprise ball. When the grown-up helping you with the party starts the music, pass the ball around. When the music stops, the person holding the ball starts to unwrap it. (Anyone who drops the ball or tears the streamer is out of the game and moves out of the circle.) Every time the music starts, the partly unwrapped ball is passed again. Every time the music stops, whoever has the ball can continue to unwrap it. The lucky person who unwraps the last of the streamer and finally gets to the prize at the center of the ball is the winner—and gets to keep the prize.

Color the Rainbow Relay

YOU WILL NEED:
- two sheets of white paper
- two boxes of crayons or markers

TO GET READY, draw the outline of a rainbow on each of the two sheets of white paper.

TO PLAY, divide the players into two teams. (If you have an uneven number of people, someone can go twice.) The teams line up on one side of the room. Put the two rainbow pictures on a table on the other side of the room. Give the first person in line on each team a box of crayons or markers.

At the signal "Go," the first person in line runs to the rainbow picture and colors the first arch of the rainbow red. Then the player puts the crayon or marker back in the box, closes it, runs back, and gives the box to the next person in line. The first team to color a rainbow completely—and put the crayons or markers away—is the winner.

If you have fewer than six people on the team, the players repeat turns until the rainbow is colored. If you have more than six, you can either make a third team or add more things to color, such as a sun or clouds.

Bug Party

Have a "buggy" birthday
with this party idea.

Bug Invitation

FOR EACH INVITATION YOU WILL NEED:
yellow and green construction paper
paper fastener

TOOLS: scissors, marker, a saucer or
small plate

1 Trace around the saucer
to make one circle on the
yellow paper and one on the
green. Cut out both circles. Cut
the yellow circle in half. To make the
bug's head, cut out another green circle, about 2 inches (5 cm) in diameter.

2 Place the center of the small circle on the edge of the large green circle. Lay
the two halves of the yellow circle on top of the large green circle, overlap-
ping the cut edges of the halves.

3 To hold the bug together, poke a paper fastener through the yellow circle and
the two green circles where they overlap. You now have a green bug with
yellow wings that open and shut. Draw a face on the bug head.

4 Close the wings and write, "Come to a Buggy birthday party for..." Open
the wings and write your name, the place where your party will be held, the
date and time of the party. Be sure to include RSVP (which means "please
respond") and your phone number so your friends can tell you whether or not
they can come.

Use rubber bugs for decoration.

giant pompom bug

rubber bugs

Buggy Party Hat

FOR EACH HAT YOU WILL NEED:
6-inch (15-cm) paper bowl
construction paper of different colors
black construction-paper scraps
6-inch (15-cm) pipe cleaner

TOOLS: scissors, white glue,
cellophane tape

1 Cut six legs, each 6 inches (15 cm) long from construction paper. Glue three legs on each side of the bowl. Tape them in position while they are drying. Bend each leg in the middle so that the legs hang down from the bowl.

2 Cut two round eyes from black construction paper. Glue them to the edge of one end of the bowl. Remember, the legs should stick out on each side.

3 Poke a hole above each eye. Thread the pipe cleaner through the two holes so that the ends stick up like antennas. Curl the two ends of the pipe cleaner.

To make a colorful array of bug hats for your guests, use different colors of construction paper and pipe cleaners for each bug. If you wish, you can color the white paper bowls or add details with crayons or markers. If you decide to use colored plastic bowls, staple an elastic chin strap to each hat to hold it on. Paper bowls stay on your head pretty well, but plastic bowls are very slippery.

Bug Party Table Decorations

Cover the table with a bright-green paper tablecloth. Spread Easter grass over the table. If you have some plastic bugs, put them in the grass on the table. Use a mix of colorful partyware. Add bug eyes to the cups and plates with large-size self-stick dots. Poke two holes at the top of each plate and string a 6-inch (15-cm) pipe cleaner through to make antennas. Cross two straws in each cup to look like antennas.

27

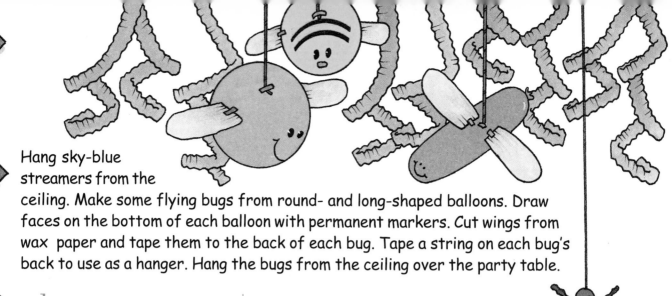

Hang sky-blue streamers from the ceiling. Make some flying bugs from round- and long-shaped balloons. Draw faces on the bottom of each balloon with permanent markers. Cut wings from wax paper and tape them to the back of each bug. Tape a string on each bug's back to use as a hanger. Hang the bugs from the ceiling over the party table.

Flying Bug Party Favor

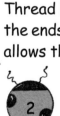

pop-up lady bug

FOR EACH FAVOR YOU WILL NEED:
two 6-inch (15-cm) plastic or paper bowls
two round balloons
6-inch (15-cm) red pipe cleaner
black construction-paper scraps
plastic sandwich bag

TOOLS: scissors, white glue

 **1** Put one bowl upside down on top of the other bowl. Poke a hole in the edge of the top bowl and the edge of the bottom bowl. Cut a piece of pipe cleaner about 1½ inches (4 cm) long. Thread it through the two holes. Twist the ends together to make a hinge that allows the bowls to open and close.

 **2** Cut two eyes from black construction paper. Glue the eyes to the front side of the top bowl, directly opposite the hinge.

 **3** Put small candies and prizes in a plastic sandwich bag and put the bag in the bottom bowl. Close the top bowl over the candy. Poke a hole in the edge of the top bowl and the edge of the bottom bowl, just below the eyes. Cut a 3-inch (8-cm) piece of red pipe cleaner and thread it through the two holes. Twist one end of the pipe cleaner around the other to lock the bowls together. The ends of the pipe cleaner can stick out to form a stinger.

4 On the day of your party, poke two holes, side by side, in the top of each bug party favor. Blow up two balloons. Poke the ends of the balloons into the holes to make wings for the bug.

Let a bug party favor land at each friend's place at the party table.

bee ball

green-eyed bug balls

Racing Bugs Party Craft

FOR EACH BUG YOU WILL NEED:
cardboard egg carton
4-inch (10-cm) piece of pipe cleaner
marble or sourball candy

TOOLS: markers, scissors

 1 Cut one cup from a cardboard egg carton for each person at your party. Make one sample bug ahead of time so that everyone can see how it is made.

 2 Turn the egg cup over so the closed end is on top. Poke two holes, side by side, at the top edge of the cup. Thread a pipe cleaner through the holes to make the bug's antennas. Curl the ends of the pipe cleaner.

 3 With the markers, draw a face on the cup below the antennas. Draw spots, wings, and other details on the bug body.

Racing Bugs Game

You can use the egg-cup bugs to play a party game. Tip a long board, table, or other flat surface to form a downhill racetrack. Place a marble or sourball candy under two or more bugs. Let the bugs go and they'll race down the surface. Have playoffs until you have only one bug left as the winner.

Spider, Ladybug, and Caterpillar Cakes

These three different bug cakes make an unusual group of birthday treats.

TO MAKE THE LADYBUG, bake a cake in a small ovenproof bowl. Remove the cake from the bowl and cut the mound off the top to flatten it. Put the cake flat-side down. Cover the cake with white frosting colored red or pink with food coloring. Make or buy a cupcake. Cut the cupcake in half to make the head. Cover the head with chocolate frosting. Press the cupcake head gently into the side of the cake. Make wings down the back of the ladybug with licorice. Add black jellybeans to make eyes and the spots on the back of the ladybug.

TO MAKE THE SPIDER, bake a cake in a small or medium-size ovenproof bowl. Remove the cake from the bowl and cut the mound off the top to flatten the cake. Turn the bowl cake over, and cover the top with chocolate frosting to make the body of the spider. Use black jellybeans for eyes and licorice for the eight legs.

TO MAKE THE CATERPILLAR, line up several cupcakes. Frost the top and sides of each cupcake and decorate the tops with colorful candy. Add black jellybeans for eyes and licorice for the antennas.

Bug Party Games

Step on the Bug Game

YOU WILL NEED:
- 2-foot (60-cm) piece of yarn for each player
- balloon for each player
- permanent marker (optional)

TO GET READY, on the day of your party, blow up one balloon for each player. Tie each balloon to the end of a 2-foot piece of yarn. You can add details to each balloon with the marker to make them look like bugs, but then don't play on a carpet. Marker can rub off balloons.

TO PLAY, each player ties a balloon to one of their ankles. Leave about 1½ feet (46 cm) of yarn between the balloon and the ankle. The object is to try to stamp out someone else's balloon bug without getting your own popped. The winner of the game is the last person with an unpopped balloon.

Ants in the Pants Game

YOU WILL NEED:
- brown grocery bag
- red yarn
- scissors
- blue construction paper, 12 by 18 inches (30 X 46 cm)
- black permanent marker
- hole punch
- ten peanuts in shells
- broom or other long stick
- masking tape

TO GET READY, fold in about 2 inches (5 cm) of the brown grocery bag all the way around the top. Make the blue construction paper into a pair of pants by cutting a long narrow triangle out of the center of the sheet to make two legs. Add pockets and stitching to the pants with a marker.

Fold the top of the blue pants over the edge of the bag so that the legs hang down in front of the bag. Punch a hole in the top of each side of the pants, through the grocery bag. Cut two 3-foot (90-cm) pieces of yarn to use as suspenders. Tie the end of one piece of yarn through each hole to hold the pants on the bag. Punch two holes in the back of the bag. Cross the two pieces of yarn and tie the other ends through the two back holes. With the black marker, add details to ten peanuts to make them look like ants.

TO PLAY, put a line of masking tape on the floor for the players to stand behind. Hang the pants on the handle of a broom or on a long stick. Two players try to toss peanut ants into the pants while the grown-up who is helping you with your party wiggles the pants around. Each person throws five ants. Whoever is the first to get all five ants in the pants wins, so speed is important. After everyone has had a turn, the winners of each pair play against each other. Keep playing until there is only one winner.

Tangled Web Relay

YOU WILL NEED:
- white yarn
- scissors
- two straight-back chairs

TO GET READY, roll two balls of yarn, making each $2\frac{1}{2}$ inches (6 cm) in diameter.

TO PLAY, divide the players into two teams. If you have an uneven number of people playing, choose someone to go twice on the team that is missing a player. Both teams line up at one end of the room. Place the chairs at the other end of the room, directly across from each line of players.

The first person in each line is given a ball of yarn. When the grown-up helping you with your party gives the signal to begin, the first person in each line runs to the chair and begins to wind the yarn around the back of the chair to make a tangled web. When, after 30 seconds, the grown-up says "Stop," each person runs back and taps the next person at the front of their line. The second person runs to the other team's chair, untangles the web, and winds the yarn back into the ball. The ball is handed to the next teammate in line, who begins the process again by making a web in the team's chair. The game continues until everyone has had a turn to tangle a web and unwind one. The team to finish first wins.

Butterfly Catch

YOU WILL NEED:
- tissue paper in a variety of colors
- scissors
- lunch bag and straw for each player
- marker

TO GET READY, cut out lots of 2-inch (5-cm) tissue-paper butterflies. It is easiest to stack the tissue paper first, then cut out the butterflies. Write "Bug Bag" and the name of a guest on the outside of each lunch bag.

TO PLAY, give each player a bug bag and a straw. Throw the tissue butterflies all over the room. Fan them with a newspaper to really get them flying and spread out. When the signal is given to start, the players must pick up as many butterflies as they can by sucking through the straw. As they collect butterflies, they put them into their bags. The person who collects the most butterflies is the winner.

Bug Pass Relay

YOU WILL NEED:
- plastic spoon for each player
- two spider rings
- two bowls

TO PLAY, divide the players into two teams. Each team should form a line. Give each person a plastic spoon. The players on both teams must put the handle end of the spoons in their mouths and their hands behind their backs. The person at the head of each line puts a spider ring in the spoon. When the grown-up helping you with your party gives the signal "Go," the first players must pass the spider ring from their spoons to the spoons of the players behind them in line. If someone drops the spider, it has to go back to the beginning of the line. The first team to pass the spider from the beginning to the end of the line is the winner.

If you have an uneven number of people on one of the teams, after passing the spider, the person at the head of the line should go to the end of the line and be the last person, too.

Puppet Party

Would you like to make your birthday a "Puppet Party"? Here's how!

Puppet Invitation

date
time
address
R.S.V.P.

Come to a "Puppet" birthday party for... Chris

FOR EACH INVITATION YOU WILL NEED:
envelope
straw
pink, blue, and red construction paper
craft feather
TOOLS: markers, scissors, glue

 1. Seal the envelope. Cut one short side open. Cut a small triangular piece out of the center of the opposite side. The puppet will pop out of the open side.

 2. To make the puppet's body, cut two blue paper triangles, about half as long as the envelope, but not as wide. Cut hands and a round head from pink paper. Cut a red triangle-shaped hat.

 3. Put the end of the straw between the triangles and glue them together. Slide one of the puppet's hands between the triangles on each side. Glue on the head and the hat. Glue a craft feather to the hat. Let the puppet dry.

 4. Draw a face on the puppet with markers. On the envelope, write, "Come to a Puppet Birthday Party for . . ." and your name. On the body of the puppet, write when and where the party will be held. Also write RSVP (which means "please respond") and your phone number.

 5. Slide the puppet into the envelope so that the straw sticks out the bottom hole. To pop the puppet out of the envelope, push the straw up.

If you need to mail your invitations, send them in oversized envelopes.

Pinocchio Party Hat

FOR EACH HAT YOU WILL NEED:
construction paper in bright color, 12 by 18 inches
  (30 X 46 cm)
colorful craft feather

TOOLS: scissors, cellophane tape, marker,
dinner plate

 Put the dinner plate near the right edge of
the construction paper and trace around it.
Move the plate to the left about 2 inches (5 cm)
and trace around the plate again. Cut around the outermost
traced lines to get an elongated circle.

 Cut a slit from one side to the center of the hat. Fold the paper
into a cone shape and tape the cut edges to hold it together. The
longer side of the circle will be the back of the hat.

 Cut two ½-inch (1.25-cm) slits in one side of the hat about ½ inch apart. Slip a colorful feather through the slits to decorate the hat.

Make a hat for yourself and each of your guests, using lots of different bright colors of
construction paper and feathers.

Puppet Party Table Decorations

Cover the table with a bright-colored paper cloth.
Use a mix of brightly colored partyware to
create a festive look.

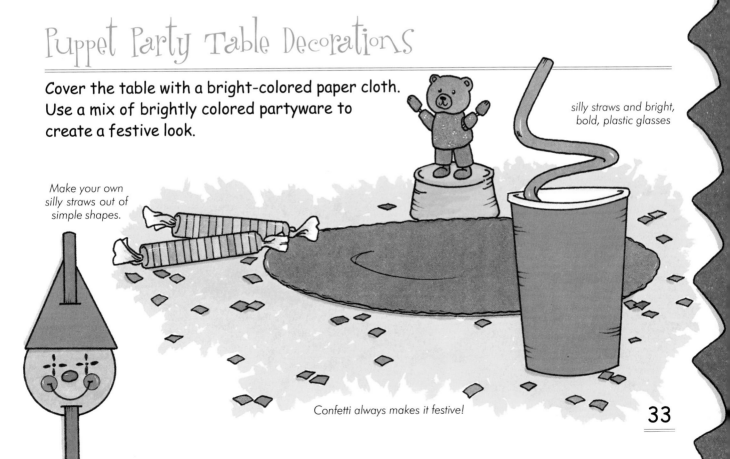

*silly straws and bright,
bold, plastic glasses*

*Make your own
silly straws out of
simple shapes.*

Confetti always makes it festive!

Hang a mix of brightly colored streamers from the ceiling. If you own any marionettes, hang them among the streamers. If you don't have any, tie string to the arms and legs of dolls or stuffed animals and hang them from the ceiling to look like marionettes.

Bag Puppet Party Favor

fun shape clacker

FOR EACH FAVOR YOU WILL NEED:
lunch bag
construction paper in bright colors
yarn in bright colors

TOOLS: scissors, white glue, hole punch

1. Fold a piece of construction paper and cut a mouth to fit in the fold at the bottom of the bag, making it as wide as the bag. Glue the mouth in the fold.

2. Cut eyes from construction paper and glue them on the bag bottom above the mouth.

3. Cut snips of brightly colored yarn. Glue the yarn around the eyes for hair.

4. Cut buttons, bows, or whatever you want to decorate the body of the puppet. Glue them in place.

5. Fill the bag puppet with candy and prizes. Fold back both layers of the opening of the bag. Punch a hole in the folded edge and run a piece of yarn through the hole. Tie the yarn in a bow to hold the bag closed.

Make these puppets using lots of different colors so your table will look wonderful.

safety pops

pencil-topper puppets

star-shaped sunglasses

Tennis Ball Puppet Party Craft

FOR EACH PUPPET YOU WILL NEED:
old tennis ball

TOOLS: permanent markers

1. Ask an adult to cut a 2-inch (5-cm) slit across each ball.

2. Make a sample puppet ahead of time to have ready to show your guests what they will be making. Use the markers to draw a mouth around the cut in the ball. Draw eyes and hair above the mouth.

3. To make the puppet talk just squeeze the ball on each side of the mouth, and the mouth will open and close.

Tennis Ball Puppet Game

You can use the tennis ball puppet to play a game. Spread lots of unpopped popcorn kernels on a large tray or table. Have everyone playing the game gather around the popcorn kernels with their own puppets. When the grown-up who is helping with your party says "Go," everyone uses their puppets to try to pick up as many popcorn kernels as possible. This can be tricky. The first mouthful goes into the puppet very easily, but as you try to pick up more, the kernels already in the puppet tend to fall out. After one minute, the adult says "Stop," and the guest who has the puppet with the most kernels in it is the winner.

pencil clip-ons

Puppet Cake

Make an angel food or bundt cake and frost as you wish. The puppet is made from two cupcakes or muffins.

Frost one of the cupcakes and place it in the hole in the cake to form the puppet's collar.

Frost the top and sides of the second cupcake and place it right side up over the first cupcake. Use candy to make a face on the side of the top cupcake.

Give the cupcake "puppet" an ice-cream-sugarcone hat with a jellybean on the point.

marionettes!

Sprinkle brightly colored candies and sprinkles to look like confetti!

finger puppets for prizes

Puppet Party Games

Puppet Bop Game

YOU WILL NEED:
- round balloon
- corrugated box cardboard
- yarn or string
- scissors
- cellophane tape
- permanent marker

TO GET READY, cut a square out of cardboard about 7 by 7 inches (18 X 18 cm). Poke a hole in the center of the cardboard. Cut a piece of yarn about 2 feet (60 cm) long. Push one end of the yarn through the hole in the cardboard and tape it to the bottom of the cardboard to hold it in place. On the day of your party, blow up a round balloon and tie it to the other end of the string. Draw a happy face on the balloon with the marker.

TO PLAY, hit the balloon, using the cardboard as a paddle. See who can bop the balloon up in the air the most times without missing. Each person should get a practice try before starting his or her turn. If you have a tie, hold a playoff match until there's only one winner.

Puppet Gum Relay

YOU WILL NEED:
- two pairs of matching puppets or two pairs of heavy socks to use as puppets
- wrapped stick of gum for each player
- two bowls to hold the gum sticks

TO PLAY, divide the players into two teams. If you have an uneven number of players, choose a person from the team with fewer players to go twice. Put a bowl of gum across the room from each team. Give the first person in line on each team two puppets. Make sure they each have one of each kind of puppet so that the degree of difficulty is the same for each team. The players must put a puppet on each hand. When the signal is given to start, the first players must run to their bowls, pick up one stick of gum with the puppets, run back to the line, unwrap the gum, put it in their mouths, and give the puppets to the next person in line. The first team to have all the players finish is the winner. This can be quite an awkward task with two fuzzy puppets or socks on your hands!

The Puppeteer Says . . . Game

YOU WILL NEED:
- a cup for each player

TO PLAY, explain to the players that they are puppets and the cup that you are giving each puppet is its hat. Each player must place the cup on his or her head and follow the instructions given by the grown-up at your party. You might want to plan and write down a list of tasks before the party, starting with very easy tasks and working up to more complicated ones. The players must do what the puppeteer says while balancing the cup hats on their heads. If a player loses the hat, he or she is eliminated. The last player left with a hat is the winner.

Here are some suggestions for things the puppets could do:

1. Puppets, clap your hands.
2. Puppets, turn around.
3. Puppets, kneel down.
4. Puppets, stand up.
5. Puppets, stand on one foot.
6. Puppets, jump.

What else can you think of to ask the puppets to do?

Objects in the Puppets Relay

YOU WILL NEED:
- two identical puppets with no stuffing in the head; you can draw a face on two old tube socks
- two of several small objects such as paper clips, balloons, feathers, tic tacs, pennies, bottle caps, rubber bands, puzzle pieces, cotton balls, and cotton swabs
- paper
- pencil

TO GET READY, make a list of the items you are using for the game. Put one of each item into each of the two puppets.

TO PLAY, divide the players into two equal teams. If you do not have an equal number of people, choose someone from the team with fewer players to go twice. The first person in line on each team goes across the room and holds one of the puppets upsidedown. When the grown-up helping you with your party shouts out the name of the first item from the list to be found, the first person in line from each team runs to the puppet his teammate is holding and reaches in, without looking, to locate the item by feel. When the item is located, pulled out, and shown to the adult, it is then put back in. The finder takes the puppet to hold, and the puppet holder goes to the end of the line. The next person in line is told the next item to locate, and the process begins again. The first team to have all the players finish so that the first puppet holder is again holding the puppet is the winning team.

Puppet Shake

YOU WILL NEED:
- a blanket or sheet
- a puppet or sock for each person playing

TO PLAY, give each person a different puppet or sock. Make sure everyone knows what his or her puppet looks like. Throw all the puppets on the blanket. Everyone stands around the blanket holding on to the edges. When the signal is given to begin, everyone starts shaking the blanket. The object of the game is to try to shake off everyone else's puppet but not your own. The owner of the last puppet left on the blanket is the winner of the game.

Monster Party

Make your birthday a scary good time!

Monster Invitation

FOR EACH INVITATION YOU WILL NEED:
gray construction paper

TOOLS: markers, hole punch, scissors

 1 Fold the construction paper to make cards of the size you wish your invitation to be. If you are planning to mail your invitations, make sure they are small enough to fit in envelopes.

 2 With the hole punch, make at least three pairs of holes near the edges of the front of the folded invitation. Carefully draw on the paper behind the holes with a black marker so that you will have eyes peeking through the card.

 3 On the front of the card write, "Come to a MONSTER birthday party for . . . ." Open the card and write your name inside. With different-colored markers, draw a monster around each pair of eyes. Write where and when your party will be. Be sure to write RSVP (which means "please respond") with your phone number so your friends can let you know if they can attend.

Add eyes and feet to pompoms.

Black monster balls with eyes make great prizes!

glow-in-the-dark sticky hands!

Monster Party Hat

FOR EACH PARTY HAT YOU WILL NEED:
piece of colored construction paper,
   12 by 18 inches (30 X 46 cm)
white and black construction-paper
   scraps
small round balloon

TOOLS: scissors, cellophane tape,
white glue

Cut a strip of paper 4 inches (10 cm) wide. Make sure it is long enough to fit around your head. You may need to tape two pieces of paper together. Tape the two ends of the long paper strip together to form a headband.

Cut two big monster eyes from the white and black paper. Glue the eyes to the top edge of the band so that they stick up over the edge.

On the day of your party, blow up a balloon so that it is about 3 inches (8 cm) long. Poke a small hole into the band, just below and between the eyes, and pull the balloon knot through. Put tape over the knot to hold the monster's nose in place.

Using lots of brightly colored paper and balloons, make a hat for each party guest.

Monster Party Table Decorations

Cover the table with a brightly colored paper table-cloth. Use a mix of brightly colored partyware.

Give the plates and cups peeking monster eyes with large self-stick stickers.

monster finger puppets

brightly colored confetti and curled ribbon on the table

Hang lots of brightly colored streamers and balloons from the ceiling. Put large self-stick stickers on the bottom of each balloon to look like peeking monster eyes.

Monster-in-a-cave Party Favor

FOR EACH PARTY FAVOR YOU WILL NEED:
lunch bag
yellow, red, and black construction-paper scraps
plastic sandwich bag
craft fur

TOOLS: marker, scissors, white glue, cellophane tape

Cut off the top part of the lunch bag so that the bag is 6 inches (15 cm) long. Cut a cave door 3 inches (8 cm) high, starting at the open end of the bag.

Hold the open end of the bag shut and let the rest of the bag puff out. Fold over the open end of the bag, so that it folds away from the side with the cave opening. Tape the folded edge to hold it in place. You now have a little bag cave.

Fill a plastic sandwich bag with candy and prizes and put it into the cave. Cut a piece of craft fur about 4 by 5 inches (10 X 13 cm). Tuck the edges of the fur around the plastic bag so that only fur is visible through the cave opening. (If you cannot find craft fur, you can use old colored socks.)

Cut eyes and a nose from scraps of construction paper. Glue them in the center of the fur so that it looks like the furry monster is peeking out of the cave.

Make a party favor for each guest. With the marker, write one guest's name on each of the bags, just above the cave opening.

Make monsters using lots of different colors of fur or socks. The colorful party favors will make your party table look great!

Melted-Cup Monster Party Craft

FOR EACH MONSTER YOU WILL NEED:
Styrofoam cup

TOOLS: permanent markers, aluminum foil, cookie sheet

 Make one sample monster ahead of time so that everyone can see how it is made. Turn the cup upside down. Use the markers to decorate the Styrofoam cup to look like a monster.

 Cover a cookie sheet with aluminum foil. Ask the grown-up who is helping you with your party to put the cup, upside down, in an oven that has been preheated to 350 degrees. In less than one minute, the cup will start to melt and bend. Ask the grown-up to take the cup out of the oven. It will quickly cool to hold the new shape. If the cup is left in the oven too long, it will become flat and will not look like a monster at all.

Melted-Cup Monster Game

You can have a monster race with the melted-cup monsters. You will need a wide board or slanted table for the monsters to race on. To make them move really fast, place a small ball or marble underneath each cup. You can race all the monsters at once if you have enough balls and space to line them up. Or you can race two or three at a time until you have only one winner.

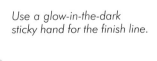

Use a glow-in-the-dark sticky hand for the finish line.

Black monster eyeballs work as well as marbles.

Monster Cakes

Bake three cakes in medium-size bowls to make three little monster cakes. Remove the cakes from the bowls. Cut the mound off the top of each cake to flatten it.

Use food coloring to make three different colors of frosting. Invert the cakes and frost them each with a different color.

Make eyes for each monster by frosting two marshmallow halves. Poke a jellybean half into each one. Put two eyes on one side of each cake. On the day of the party, to make noses, blow up a small different-color balloon for each monster. Push the end of each balloon into one cake, just below the eyes.

Monster Party Games

Monster Grocery Shopping Game

YOU WILL NEED:
- grocery bag for each player
- lots of socks rolled into balls
- marker

TO GET READY, write the name of a different player on each grocery bag. Each player is a hungry monster, and the bag is his cave.

TO PLAY, line up all the grocery bags along one side of the room, with the openings facing the opposite side of the room. Spread all the sock balls out at the opposite end of the room. These are the bags of monster food—yum yum! When the signal is given to start, the monsters shop for food to bring back to their caves. The only way the monsters may bring their food home is with their feet. Once the food is in a cave, it cannot be taken by any other player. The monster with the most food in his or her cave when all the food is gone is the winner.

If you do not have enough sock balls, make more food by stuffing lunch bags with crumpled newspaper. Twist the tops of the bags to close them.

Monster Stew Relay Race

YOU WILL NEED:
- two large cartons of equal size, filled with Styrofoam packing pieces
- pencil and paper
- two of each of these objects: grapes, spider rings, rubber gloves, gummy worms, cooked spaghetti, plastic teeth, wax lips

TO GET READY, make a list of the monster body parts and monster pets: eyes (grapes), spiders (spider rings), hands (rubber gloves), worms (gummy worms), hair (cooked spaghetti), teeth (plastic teeth), and lips (wax lips). Put one of each object in each box. Mix the body parts and pets into the Styrofoam pieces. Don't tell the players what the body parts and pets are made of. When the grown-up who is helping with your party calls out one of the parts or pets to look for, let the player feel around in the box to find it. Creepy!

TO PLAY, divide the players into two teams with an equal number of people on each team. If you do not have an equal number, choose someone from the team that is missing a person to go twice. The teams line up at one end of the room. When the adult calls out the monster body part or pet, the first player in each line runs to one of the boxes to find it. The player finds the object, pulls it from the box, and shows it to the adult. If it is correct, the player puts it back into the box, then runs back to the end of the team's line, tagging the next player to take a turn. If a player pulls out the wrong body part or pet, he or she must put it back in the box, run back to the front of the line, then run back to the box to try again. Each player must locate the correct item before the next player can take a turn. The first team to have each player find the right body part or pet and return to the line is the winner.

If there are more players than body parts or pets in the boxes, the adult can ask for the same body part twice. Use your imagination to add to or change the list of monster body parts!

Monster Mummy Wrap

YOU WILL NEED:
- one roll of toilet paper for each team

TO PLAY, divide your guests into teams of two. Give each team a roll of toilet paper. One person on each team is the mummy. The object of the game is to see who can wrap a mummy the fastest. A mummy is completely wrapped when it is well covered from head to toe and there is no more paper left on the roll. Remind the players that a mummy's eyes are always left peeking out—please!

Monster Marshmallow Gobble

YOU WILL NEED:
- licorice whips—the longest you can find
- marshmallows

TO GET READY, push a marshmallow onto the middle of as many licorice whips as there are people at the party.

TO PLAY, divide your guests into pairs and give each pair a licorice whip. Each player puts one end of the licorice into his or her mouth. The object of the game is to be the first person to gobble up the licorice and get to the marshmallow. Whoever gets to the marshmallow first is the winner. Continue playing with the winners of each pair—and new marshmallow whips—until there is only one winner, the champion monster marshmallow gobbler!

Monster Eyeball Toss

YOU WILL NEED:
- paper plate
- two paper or plastic cups
- two cupcake wrappers
- two Styrofoam balls that will fit inside the cups
- two paper fasteners
- two thumbtacks
- black construction-paper scrap
- markers
- scissors
- round balloon
- yardstick

TO GET READY, color the paper plate with your favorite monster color. Draw a mouth near the bottom of the plate. Cut two small circles from the black paper. Make eyeballs by attaching one circle to each Styrofoam ball with a thumbtack. Put two cupcake wrappers on the plate above the mouth and put a cup inside each one. Attach the wrappers and the cups to the plate with a paper fastener. The two cups are eyeball holders. On the day of your party, blow the balloon up a little to make a nose. Knot the balloon, poke a hole below the eyeball holders, and pull the knot through the hole to hold the balloon in place.

TO PLAY, set the monster face on the floor. The object of the game is to toss the eyeballs into the cups. Ask the players to stand behind a line or yardstick when taking a turn. If a player misses, he or she is out of the game. After everyone has had a turn, move the yardstick back a little farther from the monster. Keep playing until there is one winner.

Artist Party

Be creative! Make your birthday a work of art!

Crayon Box Invitation

FOR EACH INVITATION YOU WILL NEED:
construction paper, 9 by 12 inches (23 X 30 cm), in five bright colors

TOOLS: markers, scissors, white glue

1 Cut a piece of construction paper in half lengthwise. This will give you enough paper for two invitations. Fold one short end of the paper to make a pocket, leaving a 2-inch (5 cm) flap at the top. Glue the two sides of the pocket to make the crayon box.

2 Cut four different-color construction-paper crayons to fit inside the crayon box.

3 Fold the flap over the opening of the crayon box. Below the flap write, "Come to an Artist Birthday Party for . . ." On one of the crayons write your name. On another crayon write your address. On the third crayon write the day and time of your party. On the fourth crayon write RSVP (which means "please respond") and your phone number so your friends can let you know if they are coming. Decorate the other side of the crayon box with markers, or use that side to write the name and mailing address of your guest.

4 Put all the crayons in the crayon box. If you are mailing the invitation, use a sticker to keep the flap closed.

Jules Rime
1 Forty Rd
Monk, Fl

Come to an "ART" Birthday Party For...

paintbrush favors

colored pencils

Crayon Point Party Hat

FOR EACH HAT YOU WILL NEED:
bright-colored construction paper

TOOLS: scissors, cellophane tape, markers, dinner plate

1 Place the dinner plate on the construction paper and trace around it. Cut out the circle. Cut a slit to the center of the circle. Overlap the two edges of the slit to form a cone shape. Tape the cut edges to hold them in place.

2 Write the color of the crayon hat on the front of the hat.

Make everyone at your party a different-colored crayon hat!

poster paint and stickers

scissors, paper, crayons, markers, all kinds of art materials for prizes

Artist Party Table Decorations

Cover the table with a bright-yellow paper tablecloth. Use all different colors of partyware. Spread crayons around the table. Invite your guests to decorate the tablecloth for you.

Make simple straw decorations.

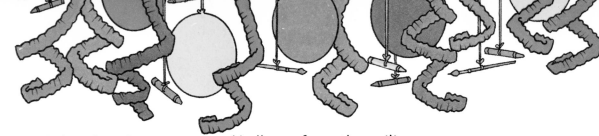

Hang lots of brightly colored streamers and balloons from the ceiling. Hang some of your paintbrushes, crayons, and markers from the ceiling, too.

Marker Party Favor

FOR EACH FAVOR YOU WILL NEED:
cardboard toilet-tissue tube
white construction paper
colored plastic cap from small-size laundry
    detergent or softener bottle
plastic sandwich bag
TOOLS: scissors, markers, cellophane tape

1 Cover the tube with white paper. Use tape to hold the paper in place.

2 Fill the plastic bag with candy and small prizes and tuck it into the tube. The bag should stay without slipping out the bottom, but you can put a crisscross of tape over the bottom of the tube to be sure.

3 Cover the top of the tube with the plastic cap to make a party favor that looks like an extra-large marker. Whatever the cap color is will be the color of the marker party favor. Write the name of the color on the side of the party favor using a marker of the same color. For example, if the cap on the party favor is blue, use a blue marker to label and decorate the party favor. Add any other type of decoration you want.

Collect lots of different color lids to make a colorful array of marker party favors for your guests.

silly mini erasers and pencil toppers for prizes

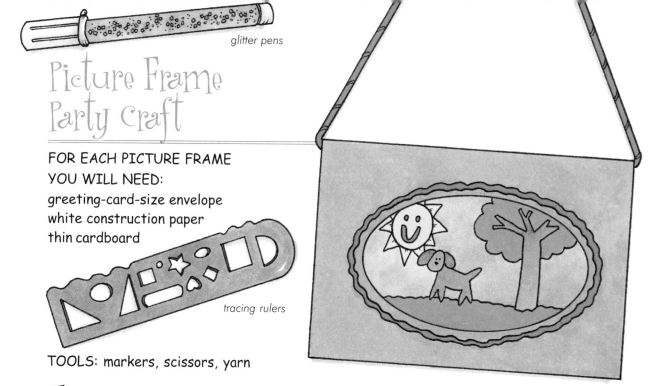

glitter pens

Picture Frame Party Craft

FOR EACH PICTURE FRAME
YOU WILL NEED:
greeting-card-size envelope
white construction paper
thin cardboard

tracing rulers

TOOLS: markers, scissors, yarn

1 Use the thin cardboard to make a pattern of the opening you want for your picture frame. The hole can be an oval, a circle, or a rectangle, but it should be big enough so that you can see a picture placed behind it. Trace the pattern on the front of the envelope and cut out the shape.

2 Cut a piece of white paper to fit inside each envelope. An easy way to do this is to trace around the envelope, then cut out the paper inside the traced lines. If the paper still does not fit in the envelope, trim off a bit more.

3 At your party have each guest draw a picture on the white paper and decorate the envelope picture frame with markers. Cut an 18-inch (46-cm) piece of yarn for each person to use as a picture hanger. Seal the envelope with the yarn under the flap, then tie the two ends of the yarn together.

Picture Frame Art Show

If you want, have an art show with all the pictures. Make blue ribbons ahead of time in enough different categories so that everyone wins. You might have a prize for the prettiest, the most colorful, the funniest, the most original, and so on.

Make sure that everyone is a winner!

Paintbox Cake

Bake a sheet cake and cover it with white frosting. Bake eight cupcakes, putting lots of batter in each one so that the cakes puff up over the tops of the baking tin.

mini watercolor paintboxes for favors

Cut off the tops of the cupcakes. Use food coloring to make different colors of frosting, and frost each cupcake top with a different color.

Arrange the tops in two rows of four on the top of the sheetcake so that they look like the colors in a paintbox. Set a paintbrush down next to the cake.

Artist Party Games

Giant Paintbrush Drop

YOU WILL NEED:
- broom
- clothesline

TO PLAY, mark out a small circle on the ground with the clothesline. The grown-up who is helping you with your party stands in the center of the circle holding the broom upright. The players stand outside the circle. The object of the game is to keep the paintbrush, which is the broom, from falling over when the adult lets go of it. The adult calls out the name of one player,

lets go of the broom, and moves out of the way. The player must run to the center of the circle and catch the broom before it falls. If the player misses, he or she is out of the game. When each player has had a turn, make the circle bigger. This will make the game harder. The adult should call the names in the next round in a different order so that the players do not know when their turns will be. Keep playing until only one person is left—the winner of the game.

Playing this game very quickly adds to the fun and excitement!

48

Sculptors Relay Race

YOU WILL NEED:
- two cans of Play-Doh
- piece of yarn
- index cards
- pen
- two work surfaces

TO GET READY, count out enough index cards for all the players. On each card, write the name of an object that the player must make out of Play-Doh. Divide the cards into two sets, one set for each team. Make sure that the two players are making objects of equal difficulty. For example, if one team has to make a Play-Doh cat, the other team could be assigned to make a dog. If you would like to play this game, too, ask the grown-up helping you with your party to make the cards for you.

TO PLAY, divide the players into two teams with an equal number of people on each team. If you do not have an equal number, choose someone from the team that is missing a person to go twice. Place both sets of index cards face down on the work surfaces. The first person from each team goes to a work surface and chooses a card to see what to make. The rest of the player's team may not see the card. The players then hand the cards to the adult. Each player's team must guess what object the player is making by looking at the Play-Doh sculpture as it is being made. The "sculptor" may not talk, but may continue to work on the sculpture for as long as it takes the team to guess what it is. When the object is correctly guessed, the next person on the team goes to the work surface and draws a new card to see what to make. The winning team is the first team to correctly guess all the sculptures.

Color Toss and Match

YOU WILL NEED:
- red, blue, green, yellow, orange, and purple crayons
- six paper bowls
- red, blue, green, yellow, orange, and purple construction paper
- scissors
- cellophane tape
- marker
- masking tape

TO GET READY, cut one paper circle out of each of the six colors of construction paper. The circles should fit in the bottoms of the bowls. Tape the circles in place. Number the circles from 1 to 6.

TO PLAY, arrange the bowls on the ground, placing the circles with the higher numbers farthest away. Make a line on the ground with masking tape for the players to stand behind as they play. The players take turns tossing crayons into the bowls. The player scores whatever number is written on the paper circle in the bowl. If the crayon color matches the color of the paper circle, the player gets double points. The player with the highest score is the winner. If there is a tie, have a playoff until there is only one winner.

Color Hunt

YOU WILL NEED:
- red, orange, pink, gray, white, tan, yellow, green, blue, purple, black, and brown construction paper
- scissors
- egg carton for each guest
- permanent marker

TO GET READY, cut a circle 2 inches (5 cm) in diameter from each of the 12 colors of paper. Make a set of 12 circles for each player. These circles are the paint spots. Write a player's name on each of the egg cartons. If you want to play this game, too, ask the grown-up who is helping you to hide the paint spots.

TO PLAY, give each player the egg-carton paintbox with his or her name on it. When the adult gives the signal to begin, the players hunt for the 12 different-color paint spots they need to fill their paintboxes. Each player can take only one spot of each color. The first to fill a paintbox with all 12 colors wins.
Even after you have a winner, it is fun to play until everyone has found all 12 colors.

Colored Objects Memory Game

YOU WILL NEED:
- large tray
- cloth that will completely cover the tray
- pencil and paper for each player
- objects in the eight basic crayon colors and whatever other colors you want to add

TO GET READY, find one household object in each of the basic crayon colors. Find other objects in colors such as pink, gray, lavender, and turquoise, until you have about twenty objects. Put the objects on the tray and cover them with the cloth. If you want to play this game, too, ask the grown-up helping you with your party to put the objects on the tray and cover them.

TO PLAY, give each player a paper and a pencil. The adult brings out the tray and uncovers it. The players have three minutes to study and memorize the objects on the tray. Then the adult covers the tray again and removes it from sight. The players have five minutes to write down the names and colors of as many objects as they can remember. At the end of the three minutes, the adult announces that the time is up. One point is given for each correctly named object and one point for each correctly named color. Colors without object names do not count. If you wish, the players can exchange papers to count up each other's points. The person with the highest score is the winner.

Dinosaur Party

Invite your friends to a gigantic celebration!

Dinosaur Invitation

FOR EACH INVITATION YOU WILL NEED:
red, brown, and green construction paper

TOOLS: scissors, markers, white glue

1 Place a sheet of green paper on top of a sheet of red paper and fold them in half lengthwise. Starting at the fold, cut out a long dinosaur head, with the back of the head on the fold. Trim around the edge of the red paper so that it is ½ inch (1.25 cm) smaller than the green paper. Open the green paper at the fold and glue the red paper inside so that it looks like the inside of a dinosaur mouth.

2 Close the dinosaur mouth and draw eyes and nostrils on the head with markers.

3 Cut a long branch from brown paper and two leaves from green paper (this dinosaur is a plant-eater!). Glue the leaves on one end of the branch and glue the branch in the dinosaur's mouth.

4 On the first leaf write "Come to a" and on the second leaf write "Dinosaur Party for . . . ."

5 Open the dinosaur's mouth and write your name on the red paper. Also write the place, day, and time of your party and RSVP (which means "please respond"). Be sure to add your phone number so your friends can let you know if they can come.

Come to a

Dinosaur Party For...

Come to a

Dinosaur Party For...

Chris Dawn
Sat. July 18
2:00 p.m.

R.S.V.P. 733-1212

inflatable dinosaur feet

plastic dinosaur eggs

Dinosaur Party Hat

FOR EACH HAT YOU WILL NEED:
green construction paper, 12 inches by 18 inches (30 X 46 cm)

TOOLS: scissors, stapler and staples, pencil, ruler, markers

1 Fold the sheet of paper in half so that it is 12 inches by 9 inches (30 X 23 cm). From the center of the long open edge of the paper, cut out a double thickness of a strip about 9 inches long and 1½ inches (4 cm) wide. You will have two tabs left, 1½ inches wide, one on each side of that open edge of the paper. Use scissors to round off the tabs—these are the dinosaur feet. Use markers to draw dinosaur toenails.

2 Round off one end of each of the two strips. Staple one strip between the fold at one end of the paper. Let the rounded end of the strip hang down—this is the tail of the dinosaur.

3 Staple the other strip between the fold at the other end of the paper. Let the rounded end of the strip tip up slightly—this is the head of the dinosaur. Use markers to draw the dinosaur's face.

4 Staple the edges of the paper together just below the tail and just below the head. Now you have a hat!

Make hats for all your dinosaur guests. Do dinosaurs have good table manners? I hope so!

Dinosaur Party Table Decorations

Cover the table with a yellow paper tablecloth.

Use green partyware to set the table. Spread a layer of green Easter grass over the table and stand the tree fern party favors (see page 52) in it.

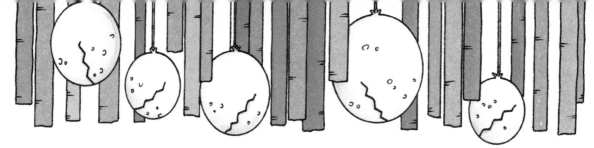

Hang different shades of green streamers in strips straight down from the ceiling. Use a permanent marker to draw some cracks on round white balloons to make them look like dinosaur eggs. Hang the egg balloons among the streamers.

Prehistoric Tree Fern Party Favor

FOR EACH FAVOR YOU WILL NEED:
cardboard paper-towel tube
brown construction paper
green tissue paper
plastic sandwich bag

TOOLS: cellophane tape, stapler and staples

1 Cover the tube with brown paper and tape the paper to hold it in place. Put a crisscross of tape on the bottom of the tube to keep the candy and prizes you will put inside from falling out.

2 Fill a plastic bag with goodies and slip it into the tube.

plastic dinosaur eggs with prizes inside

3 Cut out about 16 large fern leaves from the green tissue paper. You can cut the leaves in stacks. Fan out 8 of the leaves and staple them together at the bottom. Do the same thing with the other 8 leaves. Tuck the two bunches of leaves into the top of the tree. Spread the leaves out to make the treetop.

Plant a giant tree fern at each place at your party table.

bouncing foam rock balls

dinosaur finger puppets

Dinosaur Ring Toss Party Craft

FOR EACH DINOSAUR YOU WILL NEED:
three heavy paper plates, 7 inches (18 cm) in diameter
plastic lid, 4 inches (10 cm) in diameter
yarn

TOOLS: crayons, scissors, stapler and staples

1 Make one sample dinosaur ahead of time so that everyone can see how it is made. Cut the rim off one paper plate. Cut two pieces 1½ inches (4 cm) wide from the rim to make dinosaur feet. Cut the rest of the rim in half. Round one end of each half to make the tail and head of the dinosaur.

2 Staple the head to one side of the front of a paper plate. Tip the head up slightly. Staple the tail to the other side of the plate. Tip the tail down. Staple the feet to the bottom rim of the plate.

3 Cut a piece of yarn 20 inches (50 cm) long. Staple one end of the yarn to the plate below the neck of the dinosaur. Put a second plate, bottom-side up, on top of the first plate. Staple the edges of the two plates together.

4 Cut out the center of the plastic lid to form a ring. Tie the ring to the end of the yarn.

5 Color the dinosaur with crayons and add details to its face and feet.

Dinosaur Ring Toss Game

To play this game, try to catch the ring on the dinosaur's neck. Have a race to see which of your guests can ring the dinosaur first.

prehistoric pinwheel flower

Dinosaur Cake

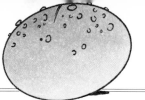

Place plastic dinosaur eggs filled with prizes around the table.

Make a bundt cake. Make another cake in a medium-size bowl and make or buy two cupcakes. The bowl cake will be the body of the dinosaur.

Take the cake out of the bowl and cut the mound off the top so that the cake is flat. Invert the bowl cake and cover it with chocolate frosting.

Cut the bundt cake in half. Set half of the cake at one side of the body, curving it upward to make the dinosaur's tail. Set the other half of the bundt cake on the other side of the body, curving it downward to make the head. Use the two cupcakes for feet. Frost the rest of the cake.

Use half a marshmallow with half a black jellybean in the center to make an eye for the dinosaur's head. Use red licorice to make the dinosaur smile, and use candy corn for claws. Use more candy corn to add spikes on the head, tail and/or back of the dinosaur cake.

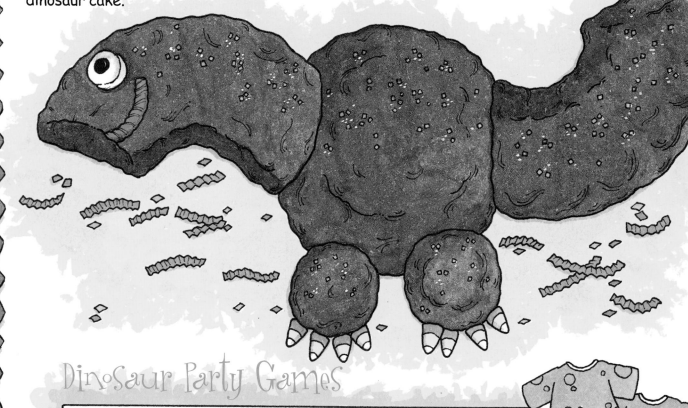

Dinosaur Party Games

Mischievous Dinosaurs Game

TO PLAY, divide your guests into two teams. When one team leaves the room, the other team, a group of "mischievous dinosaurs," will make ten obvious changes in the room or in themselves. For example, they might turn an object upside down or move a piece of small furniture or put an article of clothing on backward. When the mischievous dinosaurs are done, the other team is called back into the room. They have three minutes to name as many of the ten changes as possible. The team gets one point for each change that they find, but the dinosaurs get one point for each change the team does not find. The other team then goes out of the room while the new "mischievous dinosaurs" make ten changes. After both teams have played, the team with the highest score is the winner.

Dinosaur Hunt

YOU WILL NEED:
- one or more bags of gummy dinosaurs
- plastic eggs left over from Easter or some aluminum foil
- lunch bag for each player
- marker

TO GET READY, choose one gummy dinosaur to be the prize dinosaur. Be sure to remember what color and kind of dinosaur it is. Set aside all the other dinosaurs in the bag that are the same color and kind as the prize dinosaur. These won't be used in the game. Put the prize dinosaur and each of the remaining dinosaurs in plastic eggs, one dinosaur to an egg. If you do not have plastic eggs, you can wrap foil around each dinosaur to make it look like an egg. Write the name of one player on each bag. If you want to play this game, too, ask the grown-up who is helping you with your party to hide the eggs for you.

TO PLAY, give your guests their lunch bags to collect dinosaur eggs in. When the adult gives the signal to begin, each player tries to find as many eggs as he or she can. When all the eggs are found, the players sit in a circle with their bags full of eggs. Tell them what kind and color the prize dinosaur is so they can check to see who has found it. Of course, everyone gets to keep their eggs and gummy dinosaurs.

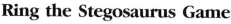

Ring the Stegosaurus Game

YOU WILL NEED:
- five pointed ice-cream cones
- masking tape
- markers
- five plastic margarine-tub lids
- scissors

TO GET READY, cut the center out of each of the lids to make five rings. Put a small piece of masking tape on each ice-cream cone. Number the cones from 1 to 5.

TO PLAY, use masking tape to mark off a line that the players must stand behind. Arrange the cones in a row, upside down, so that they look like the back of a stegosaurus. You can put the row of cones in a diagonal line, with the lowest number closest to the players and the highest number farthest away. Each player gets a turn to toss the five rings. To get each player's score, add up the numbers written on all the cones the player has thrown a ring around. You can ring the same cone more than once. The player with the highest score is the winner. If there is a tie, let the players continue to play until there is only one winner.

Hatch the Dinosaurs Relay Race

YOU WILL NEED:
- balloon for each player
- plastic dinosaur to put in each balloon
- masking tape

TO GET READY, on the day of your party, blow up each balloon and put a small plastic dinosaur inside it before you knot it.

TO PLAY, divide the players into two teams with an equal number of people on each team. If you do not have an equal number, choose someone from the team that is missing a person to go twice. The balloons are dinosaur eggs ready to hatch. Put all the "eggs" at one end of the room and ask the two teams to line up at the other end of the room. Use masking tape to mark the lines the players must stand behind. When the signal is given to start, the first person in line for each team runs to the pile of eggs and tries to hatch one by stomping on it. This can be tricky because they move around a lot. When a player has hatched an egg, he or she picks up the baby dinosaur and runs back to the end of the line, tagging the next team member on the way. The first team that has all its players with their baby dinosaurs back in line wins the game.

Swamp Search

YOU WILL NEED:
- music
- paper and pencil

TO PLAY, explain to the players that they are dinosaurs looking for a nice swamp in which to cool off. The grown-up helping you with your party secretly writes down an area in the room that will be the swamp. Then the adult puts on music, and all the dinosaurs lumber around the room. When the music stops, everyone must freeze. The dinosaur that is closest to the swamp area is the winner. To play for points, choose a new swamp area each time you play. Give the dinosaur that finds the swamp one point. After you finish the game, the player who has the most points wins.

Puzzle Party

Challenge your guests! Make this year's birthday celebration a "Puzzle Party."

Puzzling Invitation

FOR EACH INVITATION YOU WILL NEED:
bright-colored construction paper
envelope

TOOLS: markers, scissors

1. Cut a construction paper rectangle the size you would like your invitation to be.

2. With several different-colored markers, write "Come to a Puzzle Birthday Party for . . ." and add your name. Write when and where the party will be and write RSVP (which means "please respond") with your phone number so your friends can let you know if they can come. If you want, draw a picture or add decorations on the other side of the invitation.

3. Cut the invitation into six big puzzle pieces. Your friends can read the invitation when they put all the pieces back together. After you cut it, put the pieces of each invitation into its own envelope so that you will not mix them up with other invitation pieces.

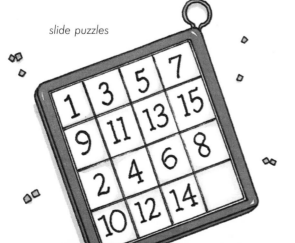

slide puzzles

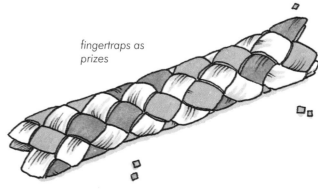

fingertraps as prizes

Thinking Cap Party Hat

FOR EACH PARTY HAT YOU WILL NEED:
dinner plate
bright-colored construction paper
tissue paper in a different bright color

TOOLS: markers, scissors, cellophane tape

1. Place the dinner plate on a piece of construction paper and trace around it with a marker.

2. Cut out the traced circle. Cut a slit from the edge to the center of the circle.

3. Cut several thin strips of tissue paper and twist them together at the bottom to ake a tassel. Tape the bottom of the tassel in the slit at the center of the hat.

4. Overlap the cut edges of the slit to make a cone-shaped hat with the tassel at the top. Use tape to hold the hat together.

5. Use the marker to write the words "Thinking Cap" on the front of the hat.

Make a thinking cap for each of your guests, using different color combinations of construction paper and tissue paper. You will have a colorful group of smart puzzle solvers at your birthday table.

Puzzle Party Table Decorations

Cover the table with a bright-yellow paper tablecloth. Use a mix of brightly colored partyware to set the table. Scatter puzzle pieces all over the table.

puzzle loop straws

cube mind teasers

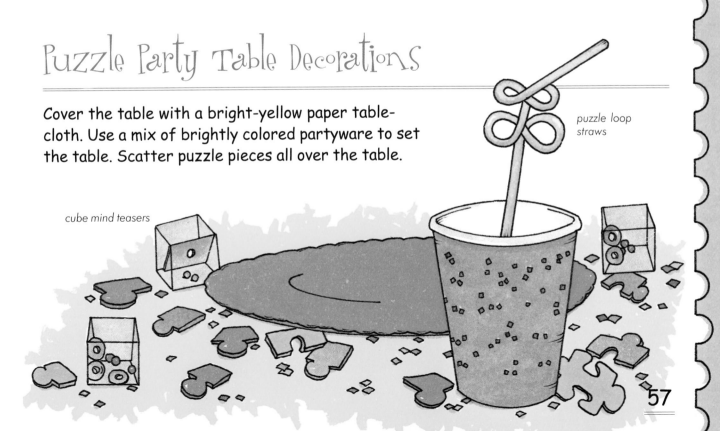

57

Hang different-colored balloons and streamers from the ceiling. Cut giant puzzle pieces out of cardboard to hang among the streamers.

Puzzle Piece Flip-Game Party Favor

FOR EACH PARTY FAVOR YOU WILL NEED:
colorful plastic cup
colorful tissue paper
colorful yarn
old puzzle piece

TOOLS: hole punch, scissors, white glue

1. Cut a 12-inch (30 cm) length of yarn. Punch a hole in the rim of the cup. Tie one end of the yarn through the hole in the cup. Glue an old puzzle piece to the other end of the yarn. Let the glue dry completely.

2. Wrap colorful tissue paper around some candy and small prizes and tuck them into the flip game.

3. To play with the cup, try to flip the puzzle piece into the cup.

Make a puzzle piece flip-game party favor for everyone at your party.

round stickers with mixed up letters of guest's name

Alphabet beads—mix up the spelling of the guest's name.

Cereal Box Puzzle Party Craft

FOR EACH PUZZLE YOU WILL NEED:
colorful cardboard cereal box
zip-to-close bag

TOOLS: scissors

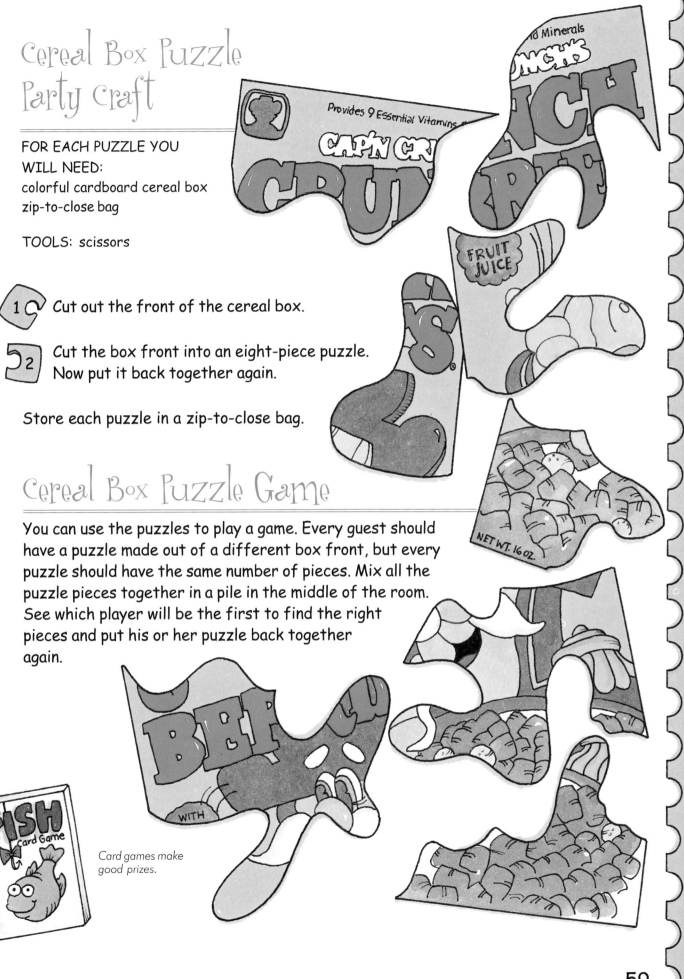

1. Cut out the front of the cereal box.

2. Cut the box front into an eight-piece puzzle. Now put it back together again.

Store each puzzle in a zip-to-close bag.

Cereal Box Puzzle Game

You can use the puzzles to play a game. Every guest should have a puzzle made out of a different box front, but every puzzle should have the same number of pieces. Mix all the puzzle pieces together in a pile in the middle of the room. See which player will be the first to find the right pieces and put his or her puzzle back together again.

Card games make good prizes.

Puzzle Cake

Add multi-colored sprinkles for color.

wooden peg puzzles

Make or buy a regular sheetcake. Frost it and decorate it with a birthday message.

Cut the cake into two puzzle-shaped pieces.

Separate the pieces so that they are about 2 inches (5 cm) apart on the serving tray.

Puzzle Party Games

Complete the Puzzle Hunt

YOU WILL NEED:
- old greeting card for each player
- scissors

TO GET READY, cut off the front of each of the greeting cards. Cut each of the card fronts into pieces to make a five-piece puzzle. Save one piece from each puzzle to hand out to the players. If you want to play the game, too, ask the grown-up who is helping you with your party to hide the puzzle pieces.

TO PLAY, give each player a puzzle piece. The players must find the rest of the pieces to complete their puzzles. They may not pick up anyone else's pieces. The first player to find and put together a complete puzzle is the winner of the game.

Puzzle Pieces Race

YOU WILL NEED:
- box of small jigsaw puzzle pieces
- plastic spoon for each player
- cup for each player
- masking tape
- pen

TO GET READY, write the name of one player on each of the cups.

TO PLAY, make a line across one end of the room with masking tape. Line the cups up along the tape. Spread the puzzle pieces out along the opposite side of the room. Ask each player to stand in front of the cup with his or her name on it. Give each player a spoon. Allow about two minutes for this game. Let the players know how much time they will have to race. When the adult helping you gives the signal to begin, the players run across the room, scoop up puzzle pieces with the spoons, and run back to put the pieces in their cups. When the adult gives the signal to stop, the player who has the most puzzle pieces in his or her cup is the winner.

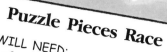

Puzzle Numbers Toss

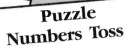

YOU WILL NEED:
- five jigsaw puzzle pieces
- large calendar page for the month of your birthday
- piece of string

TO PLAY, each person takes a turn tossing the five puzzle pieces on the calendar. With a piece of string, mark the line that the players must stand behind when throwing the puzzle pieces. Add up the numbers in the boxes where the pieces land to get the player's score. If a puzzle piece lands on the date of your birthday, the player gets double that number of points. The player with the highest score is the winner of this game.

Puzzle Pieces Camouflage Game

YOU WILL NEED:
- 20 jigsaw puzzle pieces
- pencil and paper for each player

TO GET READY, ask the grown-up who is helping you with your party to put the puzzle pieces around the room in plain sight—but on surfaces that are the same colors as the pieces so that the colors blend in and the pieces are "hidden." Use pieces from different puzzles so that you will have many different colors to use for this game.

TO PLAY, the players look for the "hidden" puzzle pieces and write down on their pieces of paper where they have found them. The players should not tell each other where the puzzle pieces are. After two minutes of playing, the person who has found the most pieces is the winner. If there is a tie, ask the tied players to leave the room while the rest of the group hides one piece. When the players come back, the first one to spot the hidden piece is the winner of the game.

Finish-the-Puzzle Relay Race

YOU WILL NEED:
- two identical cardboard cereal boxes
- four sheets of newspaper
- scissors

TO GET READY, cut the front of each cereal box into a ten-piece puzzle. Try to cut both box fronts the same way so that one puzzle is not easier than the other.

TO PLAY, divide the players into two teams. Pass out all the puzzle pieces for one puzzle to the members of each team. Some players may have more than one piece. The object of the game is to be the first team to put its puzzle together. Lay two sheets of newspaper on the floor across the room, one for each team. Ask the teams to line up on the other side of the room. With the other two sheets of newspaper, mark the line the players must stay behind. When the adult helping you gives the signal to begin, the first player on each team runs to the newspaper for his or her team and puts down the first puzzle piece. The player then runs back and tags the next player in line to take a turn. If a player cannot connect his or her piece to a piece on the newspaper, that player must run back, tag the next person in line, and go to the end of the line to wait for another turn. Players who have more than one puzzle piece may only try to fit one puzzle piece each turn. The other piece must be left with the team. The first team to put its puzzle together wins.

Frog Party

Have a "hopping" good time at your frog birthday party.

Hopping Frog Invitation

FOR EACH INVITATION YOU WILL NEED:
old tennis ball
green poster paint and a paintbrush
red curling ribbon
green construction paper
two large yellow self-stick dots
Styrofoam egg carton

TOOLS: black ballpoint pen, markers, scissors, hole punch

Hop on over to a Frog Birthday Party for Kevin

1. Ask an adult to cut a slit 1½ inches (4 cm) long on one side of the tennis ball and a slit ½ inch (1.25 cm) long on the other side.

2. Paint the tennis ball green and let the "frog" dry on the egg carton.

3. Cut a rectangle 5 by 6 inches (13 X 15 cm) out of the green paper. On one side of the paper write "Hop on Over to a Frog Birthday Party for . . ." and add your name. On the other side of the paper, write when and where your party will be. Also write RSVP (which means "please respond") and your phone number so your friends can let you know if they can come.

4. Cut a 2-foot (60-cm) length of red ribbon. Squeeze the sides of the tennis-ball frog to open the slits. Thread the ribbon through the slits, pulling about 3 inches (8 cm) out through the larger slit to make the frog's tongue.

5. Punch a hole in one corner of the invitation and tie it to the long end of the ribbon hanging out of the slit in the back of the frog.

6. With the pen, draw a pupil in the center of each yellow self-stick dot to make eyes. Stick the eyes on the frog just above the mouth.

Deliver each of these hopping invitations by bouncing it right into your friend's hands! If you cannot deliver the invitation in person, mail it in a small box or large heavy envelope.

Frog Visor Party Hat

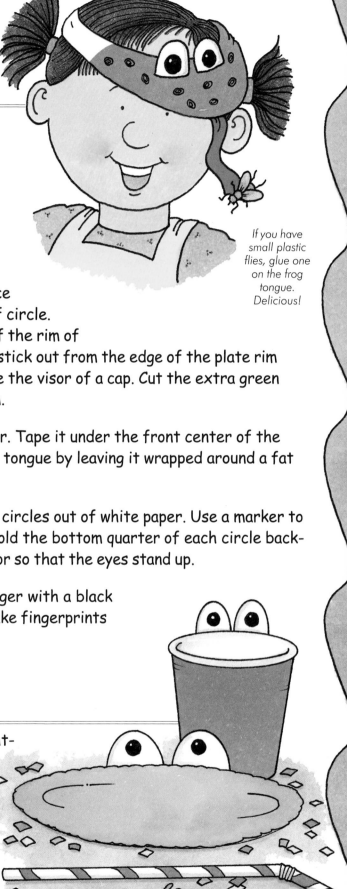

FOR EACH PARTY HAT YOU WILL NEED:
paper plate
green, white, and red construction paper

TOOLS: stapler and staples, fat marker, scissors,
cellophane tape, black marker

1. Cut the center out of the paper plate.

2. Put the plate on the green paper and trace around half of the plate. Cut out the half circle. Staple the half circle to the underside of the rim of the paper plate. The green paper should stick out from the edge of the plate rim about 2 inches (5 cm) so that it looks like the visor of a cap. Cut the extra green paper out of the opening of the plate rim.

3. Cut a 4-inch (10-cm) strip from red paper. Tape it under the front center of the visor to make the frog's tongue. Curl the tongue by leaving it wrapped around a fat marker for a few minutes.

4. To make the eyes, cut two 2-inch (5-cm) circles out of white paper. Use a marker to draw a pupil in the center of each eye. Fold the bottom quarter of each circle backward and tape the folded part to the visor so that the eyes stand up.

5. If you want a spotted frog, rub your finger with a black marker (make sure it's washable!) and make fingerprints all over the top of the visor.

If you have small plastic flies, glue one on the frog tongue. Delicious!

Table Decorations

Use a bright-blue paper tablecloth and bright-green partyware. Cut big frog eyes from white paper and add a pupil to the middle of each one with a black marker. Tape a set of eyes to the back of each plate so that they stick up over the top.

Hang blue streamers over the table. Decorate round and long-shaped balloons to look like bugs by drawing on them with a permanent marker. Hang the bugs over the pond table for the frogs to catch for lunch. (Your guests would probably prefer cake!)

Polliwog Party Favor

FOR EACH PARTY FAVOR YOU WILL NEED:
two blue plastic bowls, 6 inches (15 cm) in diameter
two large yellow self-stick dots
plastic sandwich bag

TOOLS: black ballpoint pen, stapler and staples, scissors

goofy squirt balls

1. Cut a triangle-shaped piece out of the rim of one bowl. The triangle should be about 3 inches (8 cm) wide at the base and come to a point at the top. Save the triangle piece. The opening in the bowl forms the polliwog's mouth.

2. Staple the two bowls together rim to rim. Insert the triangle between the bowls at the opposite end from the mouth. This is the polliwog's tail. Staple it in place.

3. With the pen, draw pupils in the middle of the two yellow dots. Stick the dots above the mouth for eyes.

4. Fill the plastic sandwich bag with candy and small prizes and tuck it inside the polliwog through the mouth opening.

Make a polliwog to swim at each place at your party table.

spearmint candies and green gumballs

mini-frog beanbag prize

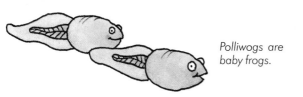

Polliwogs are baby frogs.

clothespin Polliwog Party Craft

FOR EACH POLLIWOG YOU WILL NEED:
clothespin
blue construction paper
Styrofoam tray

TOOLS: markers, scissors, white glue

1 Make one sample polliwog ahead of time so that everyone can see how it is made. Cut two 2-inch (5-cm) circles from blue paper. Hold the two circles together and cut them in half.

2 Glue half of one circle to the top half of the closed end of the clothespin. Glue the other half of the circle to the bottom half of the closed end. Glue the other circle in the same way to the other side of the clothespin. When you pinch the clothespin, the mouth of the polliwog will open and close.

3 With a marker, draw an eye on each side of the polliwog. If you wish, color the tail and mouth of the polliwog with markers. Let the project dry on a Styrofoam tray before playing with it. Make sure the polliwog's mouth is not glued shut.

clothespin Polliwog Game

If you want to play a game with the polliwogs, make them when the party is just starting and let them dry for about an hour. Give each of the players a lunch bag and tell them they are going worm hunting. Throw rubber bands all over the room. When the signal is given to start, the players must pick up the rubber band "worms" and drop them into their lunch bags, using only the clothespin polliwogs—no hands. When all the "worms" have been collected, the person with the most rubber bands in the bag is the winner.

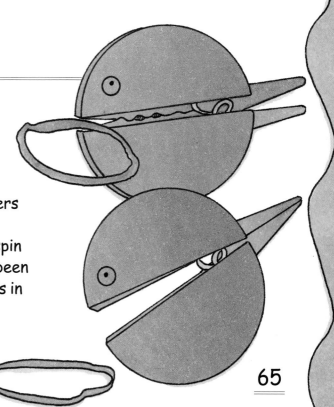

Place rubber bugs around the plate and the table.

Frog-in-a-Pond Cake

Bake a bundt cake. Make a light-blue frosting with food coloring and cover the cake.

Bake a smaller cake in an ovenproof bowl. Remove the small cake from the bowl and invert it in the center of the blue cake to make the frog. Cover the frog with green-colored frosting.

Make each of the frog's eyes out of a marshmallow half with half a black jellybean stuck in the center of each one. Make the frog smile with red licorice. Put spots on the back of the frog using green jelly beans.

Frog Party Games

Frog Stack

YOU WILL NEED:
- 12 green paper or plastic cups
- 24 hole reinforcements

TO GET READY, turn each cup upside down and stick two hole reinforcements near the top of the cup to make frog eyes.

TO PLAY, each player tries to see how many "frogs" he or she can stack on top of each other. The frogs can be upside down, but they may not be stacked inside each other. If there's a tie, play another round until there is a winner.

Frog Bounce

YOU WILL NEED:
- five rubber balls, about 3 inches (8 cm) in diameter
- bucket half full of water
- masking tape

TO PLAY, make a masking-tape line on the floor for the players to stand behind. The rubber balls are the frogs, and the bucket of water is the frog pond. When you play this game, some water could splash on the floor, so be sure to play on a waterproof floor or put a plastic tablecloth under the bucket. The players stand behind the line and take turns bouncing each of the five balls into the bucket. The players cannot toss the balls directly into the bucket. The balls must bounce once first before going in. The player who gets the most balls into the bucket is the winner. If there is a tie, continue to play until there is only one winner.

If you are using green rubber balls, add details to them with permanent markers to make the balls look more like frogs.

Hungry Frog Game

YOU WILL NEED:
- masking tape
- one or more cans of peppercorns
- ruler

TO PLAY, give each player exactly 6 inches (15 cm) of masking tape. This is the player's froggie tongue. The tape can stick to itself, so the players need to be careful—tangled tongues will not catch as many bugs! Sprinkle peppercorns around the room. These are the bugs for the frogs' dinner. Yummy! When the signal is given to start, the frogs will try to catch as many bugs as possible by pressing their masking-tape "tongues" on the peppercorns. When all the peppercorns have been picked up, the frog with the most peppercorns wins.

After their buggy dinner, the frogs might have room left for some birthday cake, too!

Frog Pass Relay Race

YOU WILL NEED:
- two large, round green balloons

TO PLAY, divide the players into two teams. Ask each team to line up. The first player in each line holds the green balloon, which is the frog. When the signal is given to start, the players on each team pass their frog over their heads until it reaches the last player in line. When the player at the end of the line gets the frog, he or she runs to the front of the line to pass it back again. The race continues until each player has had a turn at the front of the line. The first team to have all its players back in their original places in line, with the first player holding the frog again, is the winner. To play this game, the teams have to have an equal number of players, so have someone on the team that is short one player go twice.

Frogs-on-the-Lily-Pads Game

YOU WILL NEED:
- three beanbags
- three desktop bells
- three white handkerchiefs
- masking tape

TO PLAY, make a masking-tape line on the floor for the players to stand behind while they are playing. Put the three bells on the floor and cover each one with a handkerchief. These are the lily pads. Each player gets a chance to toss the three beanbag "frogs" onto the lily pads. To officially land on a lily pad, the frog must ring the bell underneath the handkerchief. If there is a tie after the first round, keep playing until there is only one winner.

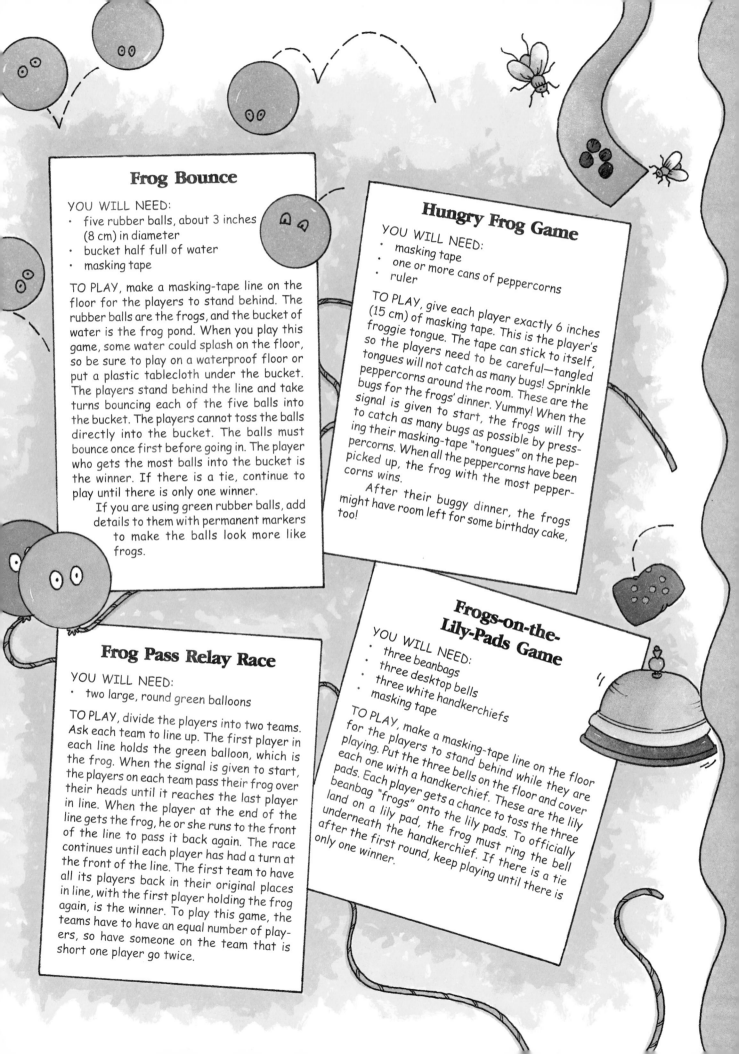

Firefighter Party

Invite your friends to a "hot" birthday party!

Fire Hose Invitation

FOR EACH INVITATION YOU WILL NEED:
cardboard toilet-tissue tube
red construction paper
aluminum foil
clothesline
TOOLS: black marker, scissors,
cellophane tape

Come to a Firefighter Birthday
Party for.....
Andy
date and time
where
R.S.V.P.

1 Cover the tube with red construction paper. Tape the paper in place.

2 On the tube write "Come to a Firefighter Birthday Party for . . ." and add your name. Write when and where the party will be, and RSVP (which means "please respond).
Write your phone number so your friends can let you know if they can come.

3 Cut a $\frac{1}{2}$-inch (1.25-cm) slit in one end of the tube. Knot the end of a clothesline and slip the knot inside the slit in the tube. Wrap the clothesline around the tube like a hose until you've wrapped the whole tube. Cut the clothesline.

4 Cover the end of the clothesline "hose" with foil to look like a nozzle. Cut a $\frac{1}{2}$-inch (1.25-cm) slit in the end of the tube by the nozzle. Slip the nozzle into the slit to keep the hose from unwinding.

Make a hose invitation for each of the friends you would like to invite. If you need to mail some of these invitations, flatten them to fit in an envelope.

Dalmatian Ears

FOR EACH HAT YOU WILL NEED:
white construction paper

TOOLS: black marker, scissors, stapler
and staples

1 Cut a 2½-inch (6-cm) strip from white
   paper. The strip should be long enough to
   fit around your head. You may need to
   staple two pieces of paper together to get
   the right length.

2 Draw black spots all over the strip. Staple
   the two ends of the strip to make a
   headband.

3 Cut two floppy Dalmatian dog ears from white paper. Draw black spots all over the
   ears. Staple the ears on each side of the headband.

Make Dalmatian dog ears for everyone at your party. Dalmations traditionally ride on
firetrucks, but remind them not to bark at the table!

Table Decorations

Use a bright-green paper tablecloth
and a mix of bright red, yellow, or
orange partyware to set the table.
Put a flex-straw in each cup. Tuck a
small square of blue tissue paper
in the end of each straw. Bend
each straw toward the house-
on-fire party favor (page
70) so that it looks like
a hose squirting water
at the flames.

*Big, round confetti
makes the table festive!*

Cut long strips of orange, red, and yellow streamers to hang down from the ceiling. Hang red, orange, and yellow balloons among them.

House-on-Fire Party Favor

FOR EACH FAVOR YOU WILL NEED:
square tissue box
envelope large enough to cover the front of the box
construction paper in three different colors
red and orange tissue paper,

TOOLS: markers, cellophane tape, white glue

1. Cover the tissue box with colored paper. Hold the paper in place with tape. Glue the envelope to one side of the tissue box with the flap open at the top. The box will look like a house with a pointed roof. If the sides of the envelope are too wide and stick out from the box, wrap them around the sides of the box and tape them to hold them down. Cover the tissue box with colored paper.

2. Cut a door, windows, and a chimney for the house from construction paper. Draw details, like a door knob, window-panes, or bricks, with a marker. Glue the pieces in place on the house.

3. Cut a 12-inch (30-cm) square piece of orange tissue paper and another of red. Stack the two pieces of tissue paper. Put candy and small prizes in the middle of the paper and pull it up around the goodies. Put the tissue paper and prizes in the tissue box, leaving the edges sticking out to look like flames coming out of the top of the house.

mini-flashlights

Make a burning house for each of your firefighter guests.

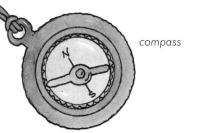

compass

Firefighter-Down-the-Pole Puppet Party Craft

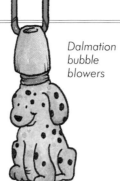

FOR EACH PUPPET YOU WILL NEED:
cardboard paper-towel tube
aluminum foil
red yarn
white construction paper
TOOLS: markers, white glue, scissors

Dalmation bubble blowers

1. Make one sample puppet ahead of time so that everyone can see how it is made. Cover the tube with foil. Tuck the excess foil inside the ends of the tube. This is the fire pole.

2. Cut a 2-foot (60-cm) length of yarn. String one end through the tube and tie the two ends together.

3. Fold a piece of white construction paper in half. Draw a firefighter on one side of the white paper close to the fold. Cut out the firefighter without cutting along the fold.

4. Wrap the fold of the paper around the yarn on the pole. Glue the two sides of the folded paper together. When the glue dries, you can pull the yarn to slide the firefighter up and down the pole.

Firefighter-Down-the-Pole Game

If you want to play a game with the firefighter puppets, play drop the pole tube over a candlestick. Just have the players stand over a candlestick that has been placed on the floor, and drop the tube. Players that miss are out of the game. Keep playing until you have one winner.

flying foam discs

71

Firefighter Hat Cake

Bake a sheetcake.

Round off the corners of the sheetcake to make it look like the brim of a firefighter hat. Cover the cake with dark pink or red frosting.

Bake a small round cake in a medium-size ovenproof bowl. Remove the cake from the bowl and cut the mound off the top to make the cake flat. Invert the bowl cake in the center of the sheetcake and frost that, too.

Add lines to the hat using red licorice whips.

Cut a badge from aluminum foil and press it into the frosting at the front of the hat.

expanding whistle bracelet

plastic kaleidoscopes

Firefighter Party Games

Find-the-Longest-Hose Game

YOU WILL NEED:
- ball of string
- scissors

TO GET READY, cut pieces of string of different lengths. Cut about 10 pieces of string for each player. On the day of your party, hide the pieces of string around the room. If you wish to play this game, too, ask the grown-up who is helping you with your party to hide the string for you.

TO PLAY, explain to the players that they are looking for pieces of fire hose. The object of the game is to put together the longest hose. This does not mean having the most pieces of string, because all the pieces are different lengths. After all the string has been found, the players must line up their pieces next to each other to see who has the longest line.

Park-the-Fire-Truck Game

YOU WILL NEED:
- three or more toy fire trucks of various sizes
- boxes of various sizes to use for firehouses
- scissors
- markers
- masking tape

TO GET READY, make a firehouse for each truck. Turn each box upside down and cut a door that the truck can just fit through. Decorate the firehouses with markers. Write the number 1 above the door of the largest firehouse and the number 2 on the next smallest. Continue writing numbers so that the smallest firehouse has the highest number.

TO PLAY, try to roll as many fire trucks into their firehouses as possible. This game works best on a smooth floor. Mark a line on the floor with masking tape for the players to stay behind while they play. When a player rolls a truck into a firehouse, the player scores the number of points written on the firehouse. It is harder to get trucks into the smaller firehouses, but you will score more points. If there is a tie, have the tied players play another round. Keep playing until there is one winner.

Stick-the-Spot-on-the-Dalmatian Game

YOU WILL NEED:
- large sheet of white paper
- package of self-stick circles
- red and black markers
- masking tape
- blindfold
- pen

TO GET READY, use the whole sheet of paper to draw a large outline of a Dalmatian. Draw a face and spots with a black marker. Make an X with a red marker on the place where you would like the winning spot to be. Put the Dalmation chart on the wall. Put the name of a player on each self-stick circle.

TO PLAY, give each person the circle with his or her name on it. Explain to the players that this game is similar to "Pin the Tail on the Donkey," except that each person must try to stick the circle on the Dalmatian. Blindfold one player at a time, turn the player around a few times, and aim him or her toward the picture of the Dalmatian. The player who sticks his or her "spot" closest to the red X is the winner of the game

Follow-the-Hose Game

YOU WILL NEED:
- ball of string
- scissors
- balloon for each player
- wrapped party prize

TO GET READY, cut a piece of string 15 feet (4.5 m) to 20 feet (6 m) long for each player. On the day of your party, blow up a balloon for each player. Tie a balloon to one end of each string. Intertwine the strings so that they are all woven together. Find an end to one of the strings and tie the prize to that end.

TO PLAY, explain to the players that the fire hoses have become tangled, and it is their job to untangle them. At the end of one of the hoses is a prize, but it is difficult to tell which hose the prize is attached to! Each player must start at one balloon and follow the string to the end. The person who finds the prize gets to keep it. If you did too good a job of tangling the string, you may need a pair of scissors!

Stamp-Out-the-Fire Game

YOU WILL NEED:
- old queen-size or king-size flat sheet
- two balloons for each person
- permanent marker
- masking tape

TO GET READY, on the day of your party, blow up two balloons for each person. Write the name of each person on the balloons with the permanent marker.

TO PLAY, explain to the players that the balloons are a fire that needs to be stamped out. Play this game on a washable floor. Put all the balloons under the sheet. Tape down the corners and sides of the sheet with masking tape. The players stomp out all the balloons but one. The person whose name is on the last unpopped balloon under the sheet is the winner of the game.

If a few balloons escape, just stick them back under the sheet and keep stomping.

Hawaiian Beach Party

Take an imaginary vacation with your friends. Invite them to a "Hawaiian Beach" birthday party.

Hawaiian Lei Party Invitation

FOR EACH INVITATION YOU WILL NEED:
construction paper in five bright colors
yellow yarn

TOOLS: scissors, markers, hole punch

 1 Cut a flower about 4 inches (10 cm) wide from each of the five colors of paper you have chosen. Punch a hole on each side of the flowers and string them onto a piece of yarn 3 feet (90 cm) long. Tie the ends together to form a *lei*, a Hawaiian necklace.

 2 Draw a center on each flower with an orange marker.

 3 On the first flower write "Come to a Hawaiian Beach Birthday Party. . . ." On the next flower write "for . . ." and your name. On the third flower write the day and the time of your party. On the fourth flower write where your party will be. On the last flower write RSVP (which means "please respond") and your phone number so your friends can let you know if they can come.

Make a Hawaiian lei invitation for each friend you want to ask to your birthday party.

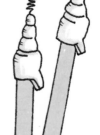

fish pencil toppers

neon-colored pony beads

Volcano Party Hat

FOR EACH HAT YOU WILL NEED:
brown construction paper
red tissue paper

TOOLS: marker, scissors, cellophane tape, dinner plate, red or orange glitter glue

1 Place the dinner plate on the brown paper and trace around it. Cut out the traced circle. Cut a slit from the edge of the circle to the center.

2 Overlap the two cut edges of the slit to form a cone-shaped hat. Tape the edges to hold them in place.

3 Cut the tip of the cone off the hat. Cut a 7-inch (18-cm) square out of red tissue paper. Tuck the center of the tissue paper into the opening at the tip of the hat. The red paper will look like hot lava shooting out of the volcano hat. Tape the tissue paper in place inside the hat.

4 Put a few streaks of glitter glue down the hat to look like running lava.

Make an erupting volcano hat for each person who will be at your party table.

Beach Party Table Decorations

beach balls

Cover the table with a blue paper tablecloth. Set the table with bright-yellow partyware. Cover the table with a variety of seashells and gummy fish.

Put a flexi-straw in each party cup. Make each straw into a fishing pole by tying a piece of string to the top end. Tie a gummy fish to the other end of the string.

sticky starfish

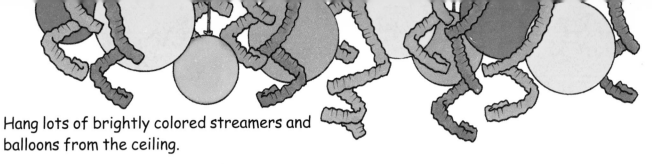

Hang lots of brightly colored streamers and balloons from the ceiling.

Hungry Fish Party Favor

FOR EACH PARTY FAVOR YOU WILL NEED:
two brightly colored plastic bowls, 6 inches (15 cm) in diameter
two hole reinforcements
gummy worm

TOOLS: stapler and staples, scissors

1. Cut a triangle-shaped piece out of the rim of one bowl. The triangle should be about 2 inches (5 cm) wide at the base and come to a point at the top. Use the triangle piece you cut out as a pattern to cut an identical triangle out of the other bowl. Save one of the triangle pieces.

2. Put one bowl on top of the other. Line up the triangle-shaped openings to form a mouth for the fish. Staple the rims of the two bowls together. Staple one of the triangle pieces between the bowls at the opposite side from the mouth. This is the fish's tail.

3. Stick a hole reinforcement on each side of the fish just above the mouth to make the fish's eyes.

4. Fill the fish with candy and small prizes. Hang a gummy worm out of the mouth of the fish as bait. Yummy!

Make party favor fish of many different colors to give your table a festive look.

paper parasols

mini-erasers

bubbles!

Hawaiian Lei Party Craft

FOR EACH LEI YOU WILL NEED:
blue, yellow, pink, and green Styrofoam egg cartons
yellow yarn

TOOLS: hairpin, scissors, pen

1 For each lei cut about 20 egg cups from the four colors of egg cartons.

2 Cut a 3-foot (90-cm) length of yarn. Put one end of the yarn through the bend in the hairpin. Using the hairpin like a needle, thread the egg cups onto the yarn. These are the flowers in the lei. To keep all the flowers facing in the same direction, be sure to thread the yarn through one side of the bottom of the egg cup and then out through the opposite side. Tie the ends of the yarn, and the lei is ready to wear.

3 If you're going to play the Hawaiian Lei Game, have each guest write his or her name on one of the flowers

Hawaiian Lei Game

If you want to play a game with the leis, ask everyone to stand in a circle. The birthday person—you—sits in the middle of the circle. When the grown-up who is helping you with your party starts the music, your guests walk around you in a circle. When the music stops, everyone tries to toss a lei over your head. Whoever misses drops out of the game. Keep playing until there is one winner.

Hawaiian Lei Cake

tropical keychains

Bake a dozen or more cupcakes—one for each guest at your party. Frost them in whatever colors you wish.

Decorate the tops with candies so that the cupcakes look like flowers. Jellybeans work well for the centers, and gummy Lifesavers work well for the petals.

Arrange the flower cupcakes in a large circle. Put sticks of red licorice in between each cupcake to make the cupcakes look like a string of flowers.

brightly colored Lifesavers

Place some paper leaves around for fun.

Hawaiian Party Games

The Hula Balancing Game

YOU WILL NEED:
- Hawaiian music
- paper plate for each player

TO PLAY, give each player a paper plate. The object of the game is to see who can do the hula dance for the longest amount of time, while balancing the plate on his or her head.

When the grown-up helping you with your party starts the music, the players put the plates on top of their heads and start to dance. When a paper plate falls off someone's head, that player must immediately sit down on the floor. The last hula dancer is the winner of the game.

Coconut Bowling

YOU WILL NEED:
- a coconut (or a ball)
- 10 cardboard paper-towel tubes
- green tissue paper
- scissors
- marker
- masking tape
- old blanket or bedspread

TO GET READY, cut ten 8-inch (20-cm) squares of tissue paper. Tuck a square in the top of each tube to make ten palm trees. Write a number from 1 to 10 on each tree with a marker.

TO PLAY, make a line on the floor with masking tape that the players must stand behind while playing. Set the palm trees in a triangular pattern, just like bowling pins, with the lowest number in front and the highest in back. If you are using a coconut to play the game indoors, bunch up an old blanket or bedspread and place it along the wall behind the "palm trees." A coconut is very hard, and it might chip the wall. Each player stands behind the line and takes a turn rolling the coconut at the palm trees to see how many he or she can knock down. Add up the numbers on the knocked-down trees to get the player's score. The player with the highest score is the winner. If there is a tie, the tied players continue to play until there is one winner.

Ring the Volcanoes

YOU WILL NEED:
- five pointed ice-cream cones
- red tissue paper
- five plastic lids
- masking tape
- scissors
- marker
- pencil

TO GET READY, break the point off each of the ice-cream cones. Cut five 3-inch (8-cm) squares of red tissue paper. Tuck a square of tissue into the top of each cone. The cones will look like volcanoes with red-hot lava shooting out of them. Push the tissue partway into the hole in each cone with the eraser end of the pencil. Put a small piece of masking tape on the front of each volcano. Write a number from 1 to 5 on each. To make rings, cut the centers out of each of the lids.

TO PLAY, arrange the volcanoes in a row. Put the volcanoes with the highest numbers farthest away from the players. Make a line on the floor with masking tape for the players to stand behind. Each player takes a turn tossing the five rings over the volcanoes. Ringing the same volcano more than once is allowed. Add the numbers on the ringed volcanoes to get the player's score. The player with the highest score wins. If there is a tie, keep playing until you have one winner.

Seashell Trail Game

YOU WILL NEED:
- 30 seashells (or pieces of wrapped candy)
- 20 index cards
- wrapped prize
- construction paper in bright colors
- markers
- scissors

TO GET READY, cut a flower for each person from a different color construction paper. Write one player's name on each flower. On the day of your party, make a trail of seashells, so that the floor looks like a giant gameboard. Set the wrapped prize next to the last seashell. Write the number 1 on four cards and the number 2 on four cards. Continue writing numbers 3, 4, and 5 on sets of four cards for each number.

TO PLAY, each player takes a turn picking a card to see how many shells to move his or her flower on the gameboard. The first person to land on the prize seashell is the winner and gets to keep the prize.

Spool-and-String Fishing Game

YOU WILL NEED:
- ball of string
- thread spool for each player
- teaspoon for each player
- scissors

TO GET READY, cut a piece of string to the length of the room you will be playing the game in. Tie one end of the string around a spool. Roll the rest of the string onto the spool. On the day of your party, tie a teaspoon to the free end of the string. The teaspoon is the fish. Make a spool of string with a teaspoon fish for each player.

TO PLAY, give each player a spool of string. Ask the players to stand in a row at one end of the room and unwind the string so that the spoon is at the far end of the room. The players are going "fishing." The object of the game is to see who can reel the fish in the fastest. Players cannot wrap the string with their hands. They must turn the spool to wind the string around it. The first person to wind the string completely around the spool is the winner.

About the Author and Illustrator

Twenty-five years as a teacher and director of nursery-school programs has given Kathy Ross extensive experience in guiding young children through crafts projects. Among the more than thirty craft books she has written are GIFTS TO MAKE FOR YOUR FAVORITE GROWNUP, CRAFTS FROM YOUR FAVORITE FAIRY TALES, THE BEST HOLIDAY CRAFTS EVER, and the "Crafts for All Seasons" series.

Sharon Lane Holm, a resident of Fairfield, Connecticut, won awards for her work in advertising design before shifting her concentration to children's books. Among the books she has illustrated recently are SIDEWALK GAMES AROUND THE WORLD and HAPPY BIRTHDAY, EVERYWHERE!, both by Arlene Erlbach, and BEAUTIFUL BATS by Linda Glaser.

Together, Kathy Ross and Sharon Lane Holm have also created CHRISTMAS ORNAMENTS KIDS CAN MAKE, the popular "Holiday Crafts for Kids" series, as well as the "Crafts for Kids Who Are Wild About" series.